STRIDE

MOVING FORWARD
WHEN YOU FEEL STUCK

JOSIAH HARLING

Published by JETLAUNCH

Copyright © 2024 Josiah Harling

ISBN: 979-8-89079-170-2 (hardcover)
ISBN: 979-8-89079-171-9 (paperback)
ISBN: 979-8-89079-172-6 (ebook)

This book is dedicated to my bride, Shaina. Your prayers and encouraging words helped me believe this book was possible. Thank you.

TABLE OF CONTENTS

Section 4. Identity

Section 5. Direction

Section 6. Endurance

INTRODUCTION:
FIND YOUR STRIDE

I have a friend who is a competitive distance runner, and he's always wanted to turn me into one as well. Since the day I met him, Chris has always been a catalyst for physical activity—calling me out to do something with him. Most of the time, the activity involves some amount of pain and corresponding ice packs. It's never quite as simple or easy as it's made out to be. Case in point, he signed us up for a race a while back, and I trained for it to prepare. Halfway through the race, he divulged that he "accidentally" booked us for a race twice as long as he had originally told me it was. A six-year-old passed us, along with a seventy-six-year-old. I'd have killed him if I could have caught him. Then, he yelled back to me that there were cinnamon rolls at the end, and we both found a second wind. Fixing our eyes on the baked goods, we persevered. After the escapade, I swore I wouldn't run with him again.

Yet, a few months later, we were at his place in downtown Chicago, and he suggested we try a run again. This time, the jog was along the lakefront in Chicago, and Chris assured me he had set up a very tame route for us. I begrudgingly obliged. A couple of miles in, he gracefully sailed with ease through the air, his breathing in synch with his movement—seemingly effortless, like a cheetah, gloriously efficient.

Cheetah probably wouldn't be the animal I'd use to describe what I look like while running. A better visual is probably an angry orangutan—awkward and contorted, grunting with rage, but slightly less hairy. My physical therapist told me that running wasn't the best idea for me, yet here I was, trying again. Chris was determined to transform me into a runner, but every step hurt more than the last. We got out to the rocky lakefront to find a few staircases up to a café. I saw breakfast and a reprieve from the torture. Chris saw weighted squats and stair climbs. I grumbled under my out-of-breath breath.

Continuing after our "break," we started jogging back. Eventually, we both realized the "grit your teeth and pound the pavement" model wasn't working very well; Chris came up with a new idea—something called "fartleks." If you're not a runner (which I most certainly am not), maybe you look at that word, and it makes you giggle. You're not alone. Me, too. It's hilarious.

It took me a while to finally stop laughing and catch my breath enough to ask him what in the world a fartlek was. He explained. Apparently, it's a form of training to help runners build their speed and endurance. It's essentially interval training—faster speed for a short duration, then slower (or, in my case, extremely slow) for a while to catch your breath, then fast again. Chris was careful to add that for me, the goal wasn't to sprint; the goal was to *find my stride.* Chris would jog behind me and watch the length of my steps. "Too fast!" he'd yell. "Too slow!" Too slow made my knees hurt. Too fast made everything else hurt. We tried it repeatedly until he eventually shouted, "That's it!" I had found the stride length that worked best for me. It was apparently so evident that it could even be seen by my coach behind me. My body moved through the air with ease. The pain was gone.

Yes, it was only for thirty seconds. But for those thirty seconds, it was glorious. It felt like *I was made for this.* Chris was thrilled. I was also thrilled (mostly because we were done). We finished our jog; I hung up my running shoes and put an end to my running career then and there. The way I figured, I should end on a high note!

Have you ever noticed that the same thing happens when it comes to our influence in the world? Each of us is designed for influence, yet most of us never fully find our stride. We tragically grind it out day after day, doing the things we think we *should* or what we believe others expect of us, but we never reach that "made for this" moment. Over the years, I've met with hundreds of individuals who articulate the same thing, "I feel like I'm made for something more." We crave deeper meaning and influence in our lives, yet we feel stuck—like it's ever so slightly out of our reach. This gut-level feeling is the basis for this book; as it turns out, scripture has quite a bit to say about the topic. This book seeks to help you find and embrace your more. Two foundational beliefs shape our approach here: 1) each of us is made for action, and 2) each of us is designed *uniquely* for action.

To start, we must understand that movement is essential to following Jesus. Each encounter Jesus had in the Gospels always involved transforming their steps. To the disciples, it was, "Come follow me." To the paralytic, "Get up and walk." The great temptation of religion is to believe that we can subscribe to a list of certain doctrines and then carry on with our lives unchanged. That's never been Jesus's offer. His offer is to transform our steps. If that's not the case, then we should double-check who we're following—maybe it's not Him. When you follow Jesus, your life is on the table. We understand that to follow Jesus requires action, but *how* we take action matters. What should that movement look like? Is it all uniform, with everyone doing the same thing in the same way—like marching soldiers or mindless minions? Certainly not. Again, scripture offers an answer for us.

Ephesians 2:10 says, "We are His *handiwork*, created in Christ Jesus to do good works, which He has prepared in advance for us to do."

One of the essential beliefs we need to carry as followers of Jesus is that we are *uniquely* designed on purpose. Each of us is creatively designed to influence the world. This means that "calling" is not just for those who serve in professional ministry as pastors. We are all called according to our unique skills for specific influence in the world. We are made for deeper things, and our individuality/uniqueness is a vital component of that. The original word used for "handiwork" is "poema," from which we get the word "poetry." Think about that; we are poetry—uniquely created masterworks of art designed to bring good and hope into the world.

What are the good works that Ephesians 2:10 speaks of? This extends far beyond just our careers, though it certainly includes them. For the sake of our discussion, consider any interactions with others as part of the good works He's prepared in advance for you to do. This will include your career, volunteerism, relationships, parenting, and neighboring. Good works are always for the benefit of others, and as a unique poem to the world, God designed you to bring good to others.

Here's the problem: Most of us are paralyzed in this process. We may *want* to move with purpose and influence in the world, so it's not because of a lack of interest. Instead, it's often that we just can't figure out how to move forward. We need someone to get us up and moving toward the goal of influence. We need a catalyst. We all need a Chris—the guy who urges us to get up off the couch, lace up our sneakers, and find our stride. Chris is unapologetic in his invitation to lead me into the next exercise adventure because he knows about the danger of inertia. Inertia is the tendency of an item (or person) at rest to stay at rest unless a catalyst brings it to

action. Inertia is the greatest source of our paralysis. There are a million things to distract us from what God has made us for. It takes a tremendous amount of initiative to embrace a path of influence. For these reasons and many more, each of us has a tendency to stay where we are unless there's a catalyst that leads us to transformation.

My hope is that this book serves as a catalyst for you. There are many things that hold us back or push us off course. Each chapter of this book will explore the things that hold us back and lay out a plan for breaking through them.

If there's a disconnect between where you are today and what you feel God has designed you for, this book is for you. You need a coach to help you find your stride. When you find your stride, you'll influence the world more efficiently, effectively, and enjoyably than before. Historically, Christians have often referred to this as a "calling" or "vocation." Let's make it more practical. When you find your stride, your life will have its greatest influence in the world. Your stride is what you've been made for. Finding your stride is defining and aligning your life around a deeply formed sense of personal mission. This is not a book about being called into professional ministry. Instead, this is a book for all followers of Jesus who have secular skills, experiences, and passions. God wants to use each of those things for His purposes.

So then, how do we find our stride? Simple. This book follows a six-part framework to help you define and align your life around a personal mission. Your stride is found at the intersection of six key components that everyone has. This book will walk you through them in six sections. First is your *story*. It's impossible to know where you're headed if you don't pay attention to where you've come from. Then, your *triggers*. A lot can be said about the things that upset us, and God often uses them to guide our steps. After that, we move toward the things we need to *release*. It's easy to hold a lot

of baggage; this chapter will coach you through developing a practice of release, keeping what's beneficial, and releasing what's not. Moving on from there, we'll explore *identity* (the unique gifts, passions, and personality traits God has given you), *direction* (how to discern a direction), and lastly, the concept of *endurance* (a great many have stopped short of their potential influence because they've viewed life as a sprint, not as a marathon). Let's unpack each of these components a bit deeper.

It all begins with a story. When I coach people through the process of finding their stride, we always begin with unpacking their backstory. What got them here? This isn't a highlight reel; this is something far more significant than that. The experiences that make up your story shape your character, worldview, and values; most of us move past these previous experiences far too quickly. Scripture shows us that God gives all those experiences, successes, wounds, and disappointments for His purposes. Take Joseph, for example. He was betrayed by his brothers, sold into slavery, carried to Egypt, imprisoned, attacked, promoted, etc. It was all part of a much greater narrative. In Genesis 45:5, Joseph, in reflecting on all that had happened (being sold into slavery, falsely accused of rape, and thrown in prison repeatedly), said, "It was God who sent me here ahead of you to preserve your lives." When we look at our background—even the painful points—we must ask: "How is God's hand at work here, and how does He plan to use this?" We must assume that He does. Rarely is a wound void of a redemptive purpose. Yet, many of us tend to run from our pain, and that dramatically limits God's ability to redeem it. What we hide, we make hard for Him to use. We must offer our story (all of it) to God if we want influence in the world.

The next component of our stride is understanding our triggers, which are the things that upset us so deeply that

they rattle us to the core. This sounds so simple, yet many Christians have been told we shouldn't trust our emotions, that emotions lie, or that they're immature. As a result, we've often constructed boundaries that keep us insulated from the pain around us. While emotions can be dangerous when they're the sole driver in decision-making, they are a vital part of a larger equation. They are valid and necessary. What breaks your heart? What makes you angry? This isn't an intellectual pursuit; this is raw, unfiltered emotion. The example here is Nehemiah, who grieved when he saw the state of the wall around Jerusalem. It bothered him so much that he risked his life to advocate for its rebuilding in front of the king. Additionally, he took *personal responsibility* for ensuring its construction. By the way, this is how you can tell whether something is truly a trigger or just an annoyance: A trigger is a catalyst for *action—your action.* It's one thing to be annoyed by something and voice a complaint; it's another thing to be mobilized to do something about it. What grieves your spirit and brings you pain? It might just be that it's a part of God's design for your life.

What about release? What are we releasing, and why is it important? Most of us are trapped by three major things: shame from our brokenness, our addiction to image, and our great expectations. These three things have the capacity to completely stall our forward progress. When we carry the weight of our shame, many of us are paralyzed from future steps until we learn that even our brokenness comes with world-changing potential. The second trap is the trap of image, which becomes an all-consuming addiction for many of us. When we carry the weight of a polished image, we isolate ourselves and keep the world at a distance. Yet, in scripture, we see the model of vulnerability repeatedly, even from Christ himself. Jesus models how to choose vulnerability, and we can learn from Him. Finally, there's the trap of great expectations. Many of us carry the expectations of others and the expectations we've placed upon ourselves. Maybe we're carrying a desire for revenge or a desire to prove ourselves to others. Maybe it's even our expectations about how God *should* work. When He doesn't do things according to our plan, we often stop making ourselves available to Him. Take Jonah, for example. His expectations were that God should bring judgment. When God brought compassion instead, Jonah was enraged and refused to work with the plan. We do the same thing today. What are the expectations and desires you are carrying that you need to release? To truly embrace steps of influence in this world, we need to take things off to run unhindered. If you're carrying things that you were never intended to, you won't get very far.

The next component of finding our stride is to confirm a strong sense of identity. This includes our strengths, natural abilities, personality, and any spiritual gifts we possess. On their own, they are not enough to discern our steps for the future, but they are certainly an important component. What are the things that come most naturally to you? Churches have pushed strengths assessments and spiritual gifts assessments for years, but many of us have gifts God intends for our spiritual influence that are not listed as "spiritual gifts." The unfortunate conclusion for many of us then is that there are "spiritual gifts" and there are "secular gifts." I may have the spiritual gift of wisdom, for example. I may also have the secular gift of business prowess and entrepreneurship. I may know how to make money. However, because God must only be interested in "spiritual gifts," maybe the secular gift needs to sit on the sideline. We've made a grave mistake with this thinking. God is interested in *all* of it. Being a successful entrepreneur is a profound gift and has the potential for tremendous spiritual influence when offered to God. See, I believe that secular gifts *become* spiritual gifts once offered. I

hope to help you identify your gifts and transform them into spiritual gifts by offering them to God.

On to direction—the hardest component for many of us. We don't understand how to pick a direction to head in, so we're stuck, paralyzed, and waiting for a sign. To this, I suggest a simple solution: Try something out. Experimentation is a component of discerning an influence path, and I believe God has designed us for experimentation. Jesus sent the disciples out on short-term experiences several times before giving them the Great Commission. In fact, when He first invited the disciples to join Him, He didn't give any of the details. They didn't know where they were going, what they were doing, what it would cost, or how long they'd go for. Instead, they saw where He was moving and joined Him, trusting He had the details figured out. Most of us feel a sense of "ensure it's the right path before we commit," but God seems to be okay with (and perhaps even desires) our trust and obedience to join without that clarity.

The final component is endurance. Most of us have perfected a sprint. In fact, our world has trained us for sprinting. We specialize in quick bursts of energy that are rarely sustained. We worship a meteoric rise; when leaders quickly advance in influence and impact, we cheer from the sidelines and aspire to the same. Yet perhaps that's not God's design. Scripturally, we never see God in a rush to do much of anything—forty years in a desert, four hundred years of silence before the birth of Christ, thirty years of preparation before Jesus's first miracle. God is the God of the marathon. We need to change our perspective on influence and learn the art of endurance.

Many books have been written about finding purpose in your life, but most center around the idea of focusing only on our strengths. While strengths and gifts are important to pay attention to, they are only part of the picture. God uses so much more than just our strengths to guide us in our vocation.

By working to identify the intersection points between each of these six key components, you will walk away with a tangible sense of how God has uniquely wired you for influence.

As we begin this journey toward finding our stride, we need to begin with the end in mind. What are we aiming for? Is the goal self-actualization? The temptation can be to believe that when we find what we're made for, it'll bring us glory, fame, or comfort. A world full of self-help books testifies to this trend and ultimately leaves us feeling dissatisfied and broken. Here's the third foundational truth of this book: Your stride is never for you; it's always for the world. We are not pursuing a path for greater riches, fame, or comfort. We aren't laying out the top six steps for success. No, this book is about *others*. When we find our stride, the result must be the benefit of the world. That's the design. If we settle for anything less, we miss the point and will be disappointed. Our greatest fulfillment comes when we recognize our unique design is for serving the world, not pursuing our pleasure.

Have you spent much time with distance runners? They're a quirky, special breed, and somehow, I'm surrounded by many of them. I've noticed an interesting trend: the more they run, the more they want to. It's like a drug, quickly becoming an addiction. It's contagious; they're always recruiting others to join them. The more you find your stride regarding your influence in the world, the more you'll get addicted to it. It becomes all-consuming. Rumor has it that as you run, your body releases endorphins. I've never experienced a runners' high (I suppose you probably have to go further than thirty seconds), but when it kicks in, apparently, there's a rush of positive feelings and experiences and enjoyment. I think the same thing happens when we find our stride in serving the world. We serve the world, and while *pleasure is not our motivation, pleasure is the byproduct.* Have you ever noticed that those devoted to serving others tend to be extremely joyful? I think it's the release of endorphins.

In the book of Hebrews, chapter 12, Paul wrote the following words:

> "Let us run with perseverance the race marked out for us, fixing our eyes on Jesus, the pioneer and perfecter of our faith."

That is my prayer for you as you work through these pages to find your stride. Run with perseverance, my friends. This race has a prize for faithfulness, and it's far better than cinnamon rolls.

SECTION 1

STORY

1

UNLOCKING YOUR STORY

I used to think my resume guided my next steps; it turns out my story does instead.

The Arkansas River runs right through the heart of western Colorado, and it provides a beautiful backdrop for camping and rafting. We took our kids on a trek along the river a few years ago for a late summer camping trip. The river seemed peaceful enough, and we thought the gentle current provided a great way to expose our kids to the beautiful scenery. My brother-in-law and I told them it was time for their first rafting experience as our wives looked at us, suggesting we were making a decision that would necessitate deeper conversations later. My son Joshua was four at the time and was a bit spooked. I coaxed him into going by telling him we'd have an amazing story to tell others about all we were about to accomplish. He grinned; *everybody loves having a good story to tell.*

We loaded the kids up and buckled each of them into life jackets to stay safe. I jumped up into the front of the raft and invited my son to join me. Reluctantly, yet trying to be brave, Joshua looked me in the eyes and cautiously agreed. We decided to forgo the inflated benches in the middle of the raft and instead sat on the very front edge of the boat. To do so, we had to sit facing the rear of the raft with our backs to the water in front of us. At the time, the decision made sense because it was easier to keep our balance. In his nervous excitement, the kid snuggled up close. I told him not to be afraid; this would be fun!

As our crew of brave adventurers waved to the rest of our group that we left on the shore (mostly our wives, whose disapproving glances continued), my brother and I couldn't help but notice the professional rafting group that had just pulled up—filled with adults, each wearing full wet suits and helmets. Odd, paranoid old people. They must be from out of town. We're locals. #natives.

We glided out into the water, and the kids seemed to enjoy it at first. As we hit the gentle current, I glanced over my shoulder and saw that we were approaching a small rapid, which wouldn't normally pose any threat at all, except for all the weight (me!) in the very front of the boat. As the nose of our raft dipped down into the rapid, the wave transformed into a monster—a wall of whitewater crashing violently right on top of us. Fully submerged, I raised my arm above my head, holding my four-year-old up by his little life jacket. To no avail, the water poured over his head, too. Because we were facing the rear of the boat, he didn't even see the wave coming. One minute, he was dry and joyful; the next, he was blindsided by a wall of water that no one saw coming.

As the boat quickly leveled itself, we popped back up. Soaked. Surprised. Sobbing. "I want my momma!" he shrieked between tears. However, we were away from the shore by now, and the gentle slope of the shoreline had transformed in just a few hundred yards, becoming a canyon wall of intense vegetation and steep elevation up each side. We pleaded with the kids to be brave, stay on the raft, and continue. Our pleas didn't work.

I mentioned to my brother-in-law that forcing their continuation down the river might actually qualify as child abuse. He agreed. He paddled us to the side, and I climbed out with my son and young niece (also age four).

My arms now full of freezing four-year-old, I started climbing up the side of the canyon in the bush (which was covered in pricker bushes and wasp nests). My flip-flops struggled on the steep, muddy sides of the canyon walls. In a way, I viewed it as a penance for my questionable decision-making. Eventually, we made it up the side of the canyon and, crazily enough, found a sign explaining that we were on the property of a high-security prison. I don't know how that happened. It was quite a scene: one tired and guilty-looking young dad walking out of a prison stay with two soaking and sobbing four-year-olds in his arms.

When the tears eventually subsided, their spirits rose. We sang silly songs as we hiked through the weeds and out of the prison property. We finally got to the dirt road where my beautiful bride and the other adults were waiting for us. As I carried him out of the field and eventually into the waiting arms of his worried and definitely disapproving mother, I found comfort in one truth: *Joshua was hardly the first disciple of Jesus to get soaked or walk out of a wrongful stay in a prison yard on account of following their Father!*

To this day, Joshua and I talk about that experience. He still hasn't forgiven me and hasn't gone anywhere near a raft again, but we laugh about it together now and tell the story to friends. That day, we learned a powerful lesson: Great stories aren't about what you accomplish; great stories are about what you endure.

As we come to crossroads in our lives, the challenge is to let our stories guide our steps. While traditional wisdom says our next steps should be decided by the best-paying salary or the biggest title we can get to move up in our career or an opportunity that aligns with our accomplishments, the truth is that the best next step is often the one that's most closely aligned with the experiences we've navigated through. As we seek greater influence and impact in the world, we are called to invest all we've learned from our experiences, not just our successes. Do you remember the story Jesus told about the ten talents? A man had three servants and was going away on a long trip. He took his wealth and distributed it among three servants. One received ten talents. One received five, and one received one talent. When the master comes back, he asks each of them to report on what they've done with what they've been given. The one with ten earned an additional ten. The one with five earned an additional five. The one with one just buried the treasure. The master's response haunts most of us today. With the servant who buried the treasure, the master was furious and gave what little he had away.

While we often think about this parable in the context of our finances, and that's valid, I'm also convinced it also applies to our experiences. Each of us carries a bag of experiences. We carry positive experiences and negative experiences. We are called to steward all our experiences to bring hope into the world. The more we leave in the bag and bury in the ground, the less we're investing, and unfortunately, the less returns we'll have to show for it. Stewarding our stories is one of the vital tasks for us today.

We're highly compartmentalized. We offer only the things we want to—maybe 10 percent of our finances or maybe our volunteer skills as an usher or a greeter in church on a Sunday morning. Then, we have our careers. We have our relationships. We have our parenting. Best case scenario, we're also recognizing these things as treasures to be invested. However, what about our memories? Our struggles? Our wounds? What are the things from the past we often want to bury? What does it look like to offer them also?

To let our stories guide our steps, we must learn from them and recognize that they shape us. The three most significant ways our stories influence us are through our *character, worldview,* and *values.* A good story builds our character, defines our worldview, and shapes our core values. Let's unpack each deeper.

First, let's consider character. When we struggle with something, our character is being shaped. When we attempt something, our competence is shaped. Finally, when we accomplish something, our confidence is shaped. All have value, but the order is important. Character is the initial building block, then competence, and finally, a sprinkling of confidence. Imagine a story that only includes attempting and then accomplishing something. The hero would have competence and confidence, but we'd have no reason to cheer for him. Success without a backbone of character is not only shallow but also dangerous. An initial building block of character formation is essential. Without struggle, that doesn't happen, and the story becomes meaningless. We only want the hero to accomplish something if we've first seen him struggle with something.

Your story should build your character. Character growth might take the shape of resilience, tenacity, patience, perseverance, discipline, becoming more grounded, dependence on God, trust, increased kindness, and increased compassion. Hopefully, it looks like all of this and more. While trying to unpack your story, it's helpful to think through the struggles you've navigated through and consider how your character has been built through these events, then allow these concepts to help steer your future steps.

Next, we need to understand how stories define our worldview. Our worldview is formed subconsciously, as our experiences give us a basic framework for how we see the world, how we see the things that happen to us, and even how we see God. The experiences that define our worldview have tremendous implications; they'll impact how we view conflict, relationships, and protection and even speak into our patterns and habits. While worldview is shaped subconsciously, we can identify and uncover it at any point. A perfect example here is in marriage. When a couple gets married, they have two colliding worldviews because they have two individual stories in their backgrounds. In the first year of their marriage, they begin the work to understand one another's worldviews (and their own!). It turns out that what they've always thought was normal behavior is not. As my beautiful bride can attest, the dishes I put into the sink don't magically get into the dishwasher, regardless of what my pattern was growing up.

When trying to unlock your story, it's helpful to ask, "What has my story taught me about the world?" My son Joshua might articulate that the world can appear to be smooth sailing, but then you can get blindsided by a tsunami at any point—so always be on your guard!

Finally, we need to understand how our stories shape our values. Over time, we naturally begin to identify our core values based on the experiences we encounter. We learn that certain concepts matter, and those concepts become guiding themes in our lives. My best friend is a marine. Not leaving anyone behind is not just a slogan or lofty ideal for him; it's become a core *value.* When trying to unlock your story, it may be helpful to ask, "What are my core values? And why are they important to me?" These values can direct your steps for the future.

For instance, you may work in computer programming, but maybe you grew up in foster care. Programming shaped your competency, but foster care shaped your core values. Your values of inclusivity, compassion, empowerment, and belonging are the values that your story shaped in you, and those values should dictate much about your future direction.

Our character, worldview, and values are the keys to our satisfaction and long-term fulfillment. This is a critical part of the journey toward finding our stride, but unfortunately, it's often overlooked. As a result, most of us are generally unsettled in our vocations, careers, and even volunteer positions. Everything becomes temporary. Statistics back this up, with the [1]average person changing careers five to seven times in their working years (according to the US Department of Labor). The average pastor or ministry leader's tenure is shorter—three to six years. Many individuals change careers far more frequently. Our souls are on a never-ending quest for our truest vocation, searching for deeper meaning, satisfaction, and a higher sense of fulfillment in our careers, connections, and relationships. Yet, when considering a change, most of us spend our time applying for jobs based solely on our expertise and accomplishments and the financial compensation offered. There has to be a deeper, more satisfying, and more meaningful way to find *what we've been made for*. Unlocking your story is the first step in this process. As a vocational coach of over twenty years, I always challenge the people I'm coaching to articulate their stories.

How about you? What have you endured, and how have your experiences shaped your values, worldview, and character?

Now, why do we use the term "unlocking"? Simply put, most of us lock away our stories. We keep them hidden from others and keep them compartmentalized. It's like we put them in a wooden treasure chest, slap a padlock on there, and hide them in the attic to gather cobwebs. "If no one knows my story, I can choose who I want to be." This is the faulty thinking that influences each of us. Many of us have become

---

[1]   https://www.bls.gov/nls/questions-and-answers.htm

specialists in ignoring our stories. The unfortunate reality is that our actions become shallow and fake when we hide our stories from the world. We go to and through our careers like robots—tin men, creatures of habit without heart, clocking in and clocking out. I want your heart to show up in all you do—your career, relationships, spirituality, and volunteerism. The key to coming alive in each of these contexts is to fully unlock your story. Hiding your story from the world robs you of your greatest fulfillment and robs the world of the benefit of your wisdom. Don't hide your story; it leaves so much potential on the table.

God's design is that all the components of our past directly prepare us for a meaningful future. Romans 8:28 says, "And we know that in all things God works for the good of those who love Him, who have been called according to His purpose."

This means that our experiences (both the highlights and the low points) are inextricably tied to the good works we've been called to do according to His purpose.

What I'm suggesting is that you allow your story to help guide your steps. If you're at a crossroads in your life and want the next chapter to have greater meaning, look for roles aligning with your story.

As we look ahead, we tend to think about our accomplishments as the only source of qualification for the future. In doing so, we've reduced the value of our background to a resume. Our workplace, educational, and sports cultures teach us that what qualifies us for the future is the list of accomplishments and successes from our past. We tout our expertise. If only our expertise lends credibility for the future, we've dramatically limited the impact God may have designed us for. God doesn't qualify us for the future through our resumes, but many of us have incorrectly assumed He does. This is extremely damaging to our spiritual health and our ability to find our stride.

A resume captures our highlight reel and puts it out for the world to see, but there's no sticking power. As a person who's worked in recruitment and HR for many years, I've seen hundreds of resumes. I couldn't recall any of them. I've also heard hundreds of stories and can recall almost all of them. Stories have sticking power.

Understanding our stories sets the stage, but we find deeper meaning through embracing the pain and transformation within those stories. Let's move forward by examining the purpose of pain through the experiences of those who have found profound growth in their struggles.

2

THE PURPOSE OF PAIN

I used to try to escape from pain. Now, I see the purpose in it.

The first time I met Annabelle, it was clear she had something profound to teach me about pain. As one of the most positive and contagious people I've ever met, I knew she had a story.

She and her husband, Isaac, live in Kampala, Uganda. Born and raised there, she was one of twenty-three children who lived in the same house. Her mom and four other women were all married to one man, Annabelle's father. It was a family and culture where women were treated as commodities to be traded and acquired. She was a victim of horrific abuse at a young age and suffered in silence because of the shame surrounding it. Culturally, when a case of abuse is brought into the light, a girl is often abandoned by her family, disowned from the flock, so the shame will not be brought upon the family. Because of this, Annabelle kept the abuse a secret from almost everyone until her late teen years. At thirteen, she was forcibly betrothed to a man who was thirty-five years old. Out of options, Annabelle chose to run away—to leave the horrible pain and suffering behind her.

She became homeless in Kampala and worked odd jobs just to eat. Kampala is a rough city, and she experienced all the pains that go with that. As one of many young, homeless girls in the city, Annabelle was on her own, without any support network or help, until one day, she met a woman who took her under her wings. This woman managed to enroll Annabelle in a residential high school—a privilege that few teens in Uganda receive. Most young girls do not have the option to go to school because they can't afford it unless they come from significant privilege. Because of the charity of another, Annabelle had been given the gift of a lifetime.

She devoted herself to her studies and to dance and grew in her abilities in both. She set a new goal for her life—to be the next Oprah—and she began working toward it. She had excellent grades, was at the top of her class, and became a dancer who performed for prestigious audiences; Annabelle was a performer both on stage and off. On the outside, she appeared to have it all together, but on the inside, she was haunted daily by the wounds of her past that she couldn't seem to escape from. She attempted to lock her memories away but could not escape them despite her best efforts.

One night, while struggling alone in her dormitory, Annabelle decided it would be better to take her own life. She crushed a battery, put it in a small glass of water, and then sat down and drafted a suicide note. The minutes passed by like hours until, eventually, there was a knock at her door. A woman named Madam Lydia (a new mentor in Annabelle's life) had sent for her. She had sensed that something was going on and knew she had to intervene.

Annabelle had taken all the messages and wounds with her into her young adult life, and it was crippling her. She couldn't function because of the weight on her shoulders. Lydia and

Annabelle discussed her plans. They discussed the water, the crushed battery, the abuse, and all the trauma Annabelle had been through in her life, which she had never told anyone before. That evening, Annabelle became a follower of Jesus.

She graduated high school and eventually received a university degree in accounting. Annabelle swore that she would never return to the source of her pain. Instead, she would become successful in business and media. One night in her young adult years, however, she found herself praying for direction and randomly opened her Bible directly to Isaiah chapter 61: "He has anointed me to proclaim good news to the poor. He has sent me to bind up the brokenhearted, to proclaim freedom for the captives, and release from darkness for the prisoners." She knew the verse was about Christ but also saw herself in it. She realized that God had designed her to bring hope to the thousands of teen girls in the same position she had been in just a few years earlier. Often, the pain in our background is unique preparation for what God is leading us toward in the future.

Annabelle was sent straight back to the source of her greatest pain—this time for the benefit of others. Reluctant as she was, she was determined to be obedient to His leading. She and her husband invited two pre-teen girls who had been abuse victims to live on their family room floor. Eventually, a few more were added, then more. In 2014, she formally started a small non-profit organization called The Remnant Generation to care for survivors of abuse and trafficking. In the organization's first ten years, she has helped over 6,000 young teen mothers and girls receive medical care, education, counseling, job training, discipleship, and empowerment. Annabelle has told me the stories of the women she has cared for—often as young as six. She has been named as one of the top forty leaders in the country of Uganda, and she is known internationally for her work in advocating for abuse survivors, teen moms, and trafficking survivors.

Annabelle reminds me of Joseph in the Old Testament, who endured tremendous pain from others. Because he had received favor from his father, his brothers were jealous. They schemed to kill him but instead decided to sell him into slavery in Egypt. Upon arrival in Egypt, he had some ups and downs and was promoted to significant roles, betrayed, imprisoned, and wrongly accused of flirting with Potiphar's wife. Joseph had every reason to run and hide from his wounds. Instead, he reminded himself that there is purpose even in pain. Eventually, he was promoted to second in the kingdom, and when a drought struck Israel, his brothers came to Egypt to borrow grain to survive. Joseph's response to his brothers' visit is fascinating.

In Genesis 45:5, while weeping in front of his brothers over the wounds they'd inflicted on him, he said, "Do not be stressed and do not be angry with yourselves for selling me here because it was to save lives that God *sent* me ahead of you. For two years now, there has been a famine in the land, and for the next five years there will be no plowing nor reaping. But God *sent* me ahead of you to preserve for you a remnant on earth and to save your lives by a great deliverance."

God does not *bring* pain upon our lives; that's not aligned with His character. However, He *brings purpose from our pain* for the sake of the world. Yes, He has a plan even for the wounds inflicted upon us by others (like that which Annabelle had to endure). It's not natural for us to identify value in pain, but we know from Scripture that God works all things for the good. It takes tremendous discipline and intentionality to search for redemption in the pain that we've endured, but that's where the journey toward finding our stride must start.

The key is to commit to a transformational arc to find the true value in our pain. Pain has the potential to shape our character, but it also has the potential to stall us. The key to unlocking the potential in our pain is committing to a positive transformational arc.

Joseph and Annabelle both began as victims. Then, they became survivors, but then they transformed fully to become *sent ones*. Let's unpack this transformational arc a bit deeper.

When it comes to pain, each of us begins as a victim. Victims believe that the world happens to them, and they have no choice in the matter. Please keep in mind that each of us, regardless of how painful our experience, begins as a victim. It's a valid place to be because it's the starting point. Think about your life as a book. If the primary narrative is that of a victim, that's not a good book. If the primary narrative for a *chapter* is the victim, that's appropriate because it's the starting point of the journey. Victimhood is valid; we just can't stay there too long.

From victim, we take steps toward survivor because, as a survivor, we find healing and wholeness. The primary objective here is to find wholeness. Annabelle became a survivor when she found herself outside of her abuse. She found a passion for dance. She found an interest in and aptitude for finance. She found a voice, and she found aspiration and hope. The transformation point from victim to survivor is to find wholeness. This comes from Jesus, who brings us to wholeness. 1st Peter 5:10 says, "And the God of all grace, who called you to his eternal glory in Christ, after you have suffered a little while, will himself restore you and make you strong, firm, and steadfast."

As wounded victims, it's easy to feel that we are broken. The Japanese have a tradition in pottery called Kintsugi. It's a technique where a beautiful piece of pottery is intentionally shattered. The pottery pieces are then brought together again using gold as the glue to hold the pieces back together. These pieces of pottery become masterful works of art because of the gold. It is this way with God. Identify the broken pieces of your story and invite the Holy Spirit to be the healing glue that seams them back together.

Now, here's the challenge. Many of us are content with just this move from victim to survivor. We stop the journey there. We're content to move from broken pieces toward wholeness. While that's an excellent step, it's not nearly all God has designed us for. We have survivors who walk the streets and fill the pews of our churches every Sunday, and many of them feel dissatisfied. There's still another step to complete the transformational arc—the transformation from *survivors* to *sent ones.*

Being a survivor is all about finding healing and wholeness in oneself. God is absolutely interested in leading you to wholeness, but He's not content to leave you there. Even pottery is intended to fill a function. At its core, a bowl is designed for *service*, to offer hospitality and provision to others. What if your journey to wholeness is intended for the blessing of others? This is how we move from survivor to sent one: We look outward. Like Joseph with his brothers, we must ask, "What have others intended for evil that God may intend for good?" It's not a question of good for self; it's about good for *others*. Both victim and survivor are self-based narratives, but the narrative of sent one puts others into focus.

Many of us try to skip ahead. We want to move from victim to sent one, but that doesn't work. If you don't find wholeness yourself, you can't lead others to a place of wholeness. Find yourself in this transformational arc, and you'll see the value in all you've endured.

Finding the purpose in our pain does *not* remove the pain. It also does not *minimize* the pain. Pain is pain, and it stays that way forever. Yet we worship a God who works all things for the good, and we can seek to find redemptive glimpses in the pains of our stories. Those glimpses may lead us to purpose for the future.

You will have to wrestle with your pain in your journey to find your stride. Have you considered the redemptive value of your pain? Take the time to wrestle with the greatest pains in your life. Where are you on the journey from victim to survivor and survivor to sent one?

Many of us may not be able to relate to being sold as slaves to Egyptian traders. We may not be able to relate to being a survivor of abuse or trauma to the extent that Annabelle has walked, but all of us can relate to pain. Each of us carries pain points in our journey that, if we're honest, we'd like to run away from as far as we can. Pain teaches us valuable lessons, but emotions help drive our actions. In the next chapter, we will understand the necessity of emotion in our lives and how it influences our journey.

SECTION 2

TRIGGERS

3

THE NECESSITY OF EMOTION

I used to think that emotion was dangerous. Now, I know emotion is essential.

A few years ago, a group of friends and I went to Greece to serve refugees. Since 2013, refugees have been flooding into Greece from Syria, Iran, Afghanistan, and other various locations, escaping religious extremism, persecution, and violence. Our goal was to come in as students and understand the stories behind their journeys. We quickly learned that these were some of the most educated, highly capable, dignified people we had ever met—scrappy in every way and trying to find freedom at all costs.

Each of the refugees we met shared stories of how they escaped their country of origin, and their stories were incredible. These were people of means who could afford to pay the right people to smuggle them out of their country. However, leaving their home country cost them a lot (physically, spiritually, socially, and financially). In many cases, it cost them just about everything. They had left behind careers, bank accounts, homes, schools, communities, family, friends, and more. Some were pharmacists, scientists, engineers, lawyers, and physicians. They had worked hard for their careers and invested heavily in them, but when the chance came for freedom, they sacrificed it all to invest in their future. We can learn a lot from our refugee friends about pursuing the future at all costs—with courage, tenacity, perseverance, and resilience.

The Moria camp is on the island of Lesvos, which is close to the country of Turkey. Refugees flee from their country of origin, traveling under the cover of night. They journey through Turkey and then use an inflatable raft to cross twelve kilometers of the Aegean Sea to get to the Greek island of Lesvos. It's a harrowing journey that isn't for the faint of heart. After landing on the rocky shores of Lesvos, they try to find food and shelter. Most frequently, they're picked up by local authorities, brought into the Moria camp, and given blankets, a tent assignment, and some food from UNHCR.

We arrived late at night and waited to come into the camp until the next morning. Words can't describe what we saw inside the camp. It was a tented community built for 3,000 people and overflowing with 15,000—a sprawling canvas city on the side of a mountain where thousands had placed all their hopes and dreams. Barbed wire and armed guards blocked the front entry gate. Because of the volunteer vests we wore, the guards didn't question us. Instead, they waved us forward with a look that said, "You're on your own, best of luck."

We walked past plenty of raw, overflowing sewage on our way through the camp. Rats ran to fight for the scraps of food hidden in the piles of trash. The conditions were inevitable, as the camp was highly ill-equipped for this amount of people; the number of functioning toilets was one for every seventy-two people, and showers just one for every eighty-four people. It was October, and it had already snowed. I shudder to think of how many passed away in the months after our visit from the temperature alone. Articles online tell you that the average stay is just a few days before refugees obtain their immigration papers and can legally move on to other areas of the EU. Most of the families we met had been inside the camp for four years or more.

I couldn't figure out why it was so hard for refugees to get out of this camp. Then, it struck me: The government was receiving money for accommodating these refugees and profiting by not building a more permanent infrastructure for them. The government received money as long as the refugees stayed in the camp. The longer they were stuck, the more money was made. The injustice was simply overwhelming. This was one of the greatest humanitarian failures the world has ever seen.

We walked through the camp on the way to the metal cage, where we'd distribute food daily. The cage was intended to keep us safe from riots. A few weeks before we came, there had been a violent flare-up in the camp, and people had been throwing stones, bottles, etc. These were dignified people, but they were also desperate and disappointed people. If I was trying to feed my family while receiving tiny rations in a place like this, I'm sure I'd be desperate, too. I'm not above a fight if it means my children get to eat.

Twice a day, people would line up to receive a couple of eggs and a few strange little sandwiches. Every day was the same—monotonous and boring. It was modern-day manna. An hour before feeding time, they all started lining up. Quickly, there was a line several hundred people deep. Our line was just for women and children; the men had a separate line to protect against violence. Every day, like clockwork, the same things would happen. People would line up, and we'd begin handing out the essentials as they received the food without saying a word. Then, the horrible moment would come when the food would run out. That was heart-wrenching. I hated having to share that news.

This place was Hell on Earth, and the suffering around us was unlike anything I'd ever seen. We met a man who was a pharmacist back in his home country. After arriving at the camp and spending some time there, he couldn't take it anymore. He drank a bottle of anti-freeze to try to escape the suffering. It didn't take his life. Instead, it burned his esophagus and the lining of his stomach, resulting in daily extreme pain. His suffering was beyond belief. The conditions in the camp were horrendous, but I think what got him was the disappointing realization that the future he sacrificed so much for was just as bad, if not worse, than what he left behind in his home country.

Later in the week, we took a break from handing out food to wander the island of Lesvos. We came upon a wide-open field with a curious-looking hill in the middle of it. We moved closer to investigate. It wasn't a hill at all; it was a massive pile of thousands upon thousands of life rafts and life jackets. As refugees made their way on the harrowing journey from Turkey, the luckiest arrived here. Many did not. Many capsized in the sea; others were shot at or told to turn around. The lucky ones arrived on Lesvos, believing this would be the ticket to a new life, only to be drug into the Moria camp to experience Hell on Earth. We soberly reflected on the fact that thousands upon thousands of dreams had been deflated here on this ground. The greatest hopes of generations in search of freedom, yet reality brought suffering instead. The disappointment was almost unbearable.

During our debrief, our team sat together at a quiet outdoor café, and the silence was deafening. Each of us was in shock, a mix of sadness, exhaustion, anger, and rage. Waves of emotion rattled us, buried under the weight and gravity of what we had seen. Eventually, one of the team members broke the silence with powerful words that hung in the moment, "The people of God simply have to be here." We couldn't solve it. We couldn't do much, but we could *be here*. In fact, we *had* to be here.

This section of the book is about the next component of finding our stride, which is to identify our triggers. These are the things that elicit a deep, emotional, gut-level response from us. These heartaches are not to be ignored, dismissed, or avoided; they're intended to bother us enough to take action. A great trigger is a catalyst for action, and finding the things that trigger you is essential for a life of meaning and purpose.

Maybe you're skeptical. I understand. In the circles where I grew up, emotion was always dismissed, like following Jesus was an intellectual pursuit only, and emotions just got in the way. Maybe you heard similar messages growing up, learning that emotions couldn't be trusted or that we need to hide them so we don't lose our professional appearance. Christians are well put together with smiles on their faces, aren't they?

John 11:35 has become one of my favorite verses. It's the shortest verse in the Bible, yet incredibly profound. "Jesus wept." Upon hearing of the death of his friend Lazarus and knowing He was about to raise him from the dead, Jesus wept. Often, we grieve because we can't do anything to *fix* it. Jesus *could* fix it and was about to, but He still paused and wept. Maybe He was doing this to teach us the vital role that emotion plays in our faith walk. We need to recognize and value emotion in our picture of Jesus. He got angry. He got emotional. He wept, and He modeled it for us. He is a God of emotion, and if we want to be like Him, we need to embrace emotion.

THE IMPORTANCE OF ALIGNMENT

When we think of triggers, it's easy to think about the annoyances or things that frustrate us. That's not what we're after. Instead, we're looking for the things that break our hearts in empathy. It's not just the things that make *us* emotional;

it's something that upsets *God,* too. Alignment makes all the difference. Many of us have been distracted by fighting against things that aggravate us but don't necessarily break His heart. Need an example? When we fight for our Christian rights. We've done this for centuries. We fight for our rights, trying to defend the privileges we experience and ensure that they remain. We even get emotional about it. The only problem is that Jesus never intended for His followers to fight for their privilege; instead, He invited us to lay our rights and privileges down to serve others. The trigger in your stride can't be related to fighting for your privilege. That's misaligned with His heart. If we want to embrace our stride in the world, we must identify triggers that break both our hearts *and* His.

If you don't know what breaks God's heart, start your journey here. Study the words of Isaiah 58:6 – 9:

> Is this not the kind of fasting I have chosen: to loose the chains of injustice and untie the cords of the yoke, to set the oppressed free and break every yoke? Is it not to share your food with the hungry and provide the poor wanderer with shelter – when you see the naked, to clothe them and not to turn away from your own flesh and blood? Then your light will break forth like the dawn, and your healing will quickly appear; your righteousness will go before you, and the glory of the Lord will be your rear guard.

In other words, if you're spending your time caring for the poor, oppressed, hungry, homeless, etc., you're aligned with the things that break God's heart, and He will bless your efforts.

Throughout scripture, emotion is a key ingredient in the process whenever leaders step into a new calling. Emotion is the catalyst for action, but first, there's a pause. Take Nehemiah, for example. He was the great leader who rallied the Israelites to rebuild the walls around Jerusalem after the exile. It all began in Nehemiah chapter 1, verses 3 – 4: "They said to me, 'Those who survived the exile and are back in the province are in great trouble and disgrace. The wall of Jerusalem is broken down, and its gates have been burned with fire.' When I heard these things, I *sat down and wept. For some days, I mourned and fasted and prayed* before the God of heaven."

Nehemiah was emotionally invested in the status of Jerusalem. He wept, grieved, fasted, and prayed. A broken heart is uncomfortable, and many of us want to escape as quickly as we can from heartbreak. We want to push for solutions to fix it right away, or we want to dismiss the situation and construct emotional walls to numb ourselves from the pain. Nehemiah didn't do either. He sat down and wept. Notice what he says, "For *some days*, I mourned and fasted." This wasn't something he rushed through. He allowed himself the time to fully engage with the weight of emotion and heartbreak. I want to encourage you to pause when you identify the trigger in your stride. Allow heartbreak. Feel the full weight of the situation. Allow yourself to be present to the heartbreak—not to fix or dismiss it but to hold it.

It was only after Nehemiah was present to the heartbreak that he acted. It became his personal responsibility to do something. There's a model for us. We can intellectually understand how our skills, abilities, and strengths can be beneficial in the world, but without emotional engagement, we'll never take a step. Emotion is the catalyst, the secret ingredient in finding our stride.

If you want to find your stride, you need to articulate what breaks your heart and what breaks His. Put it on paper and research the topic. Go deeper into your understanding of the problem and be present for the heartbreak. Feel the full weight of the situation, then prepare to do something about it. In the next chapter, we'll learn how to invite God to shape your response.

4

YOU CAN'T CONTROL WHAT
YOU TRY TO SERVE

I used to try to control the world. Now, I try to serve it.

Maybe you've identified the trigger in your stride. Now what? Recognizing emotion as a valuable catalyst is only part of the challenge. The next task before us is to ensure that the actions we take in response are healthy. A trigger is *always* the catalyst for a response. However, many well-intentioned followers of Jesus have made some egregious mistakes here, and we need to be careful to avoid those same pitfalls. For thousands of years, when Christians have felt emotion boiling over, they've lashed out with force. It's a natural response, but Jesus invites us to a more mature response. I have a visual that reminds me not to lash out with force: suction cup balls and dominos. Allow me to explain.

There's a YouTube star named Lily Havesh, and she's a global Domino expert. Her mesmerizing videos have millions of views, and the elaborate designs she makes have thousands upon thousands of bricks. Truly, she's an expert. My kids are obsessed with her and have devoted themselves to constructing and collapsing Domino creations all over our kitchen floor. Lily has tremendous precision and perfectly explains how far to space the Dominoes from one another to get them to fall exactly according to plan. As a child, I never seemed to have the Dominoes gift—that is until I was twelve. It turns out that I'm kind of a natural.

Our family liked to vacation in Maryland in a beachfront town called Ocean Beach. On the boardwalk in Ocean Beach, there's a store called the Candy Kitchen. The store is filled to the brim with gourmet varieties of sugary conglomerations. After finding $20 floating in the ocean earlier on the trip, I was overwhelmed and giddy at the seemingly endless candy options in every direction. While my sisters were distracted with Beanie Babies (I still don't understand that), I perused the aisles and found many great options. Eventually, I decided on the candy I wanted and waited for the girls at the counter. While there, I mindlessly grabbed one of the toys at the counter to play with. It was a suction cup ball.

I've already mentioned that the store was covered in wall-to-wall candy. I should probably also share that they were displayed in ten-foot-tall glass tubes that ran floor to ceiling throughout the perimeter of the store. My mind danced at the thought of crunching on the gourmet creations. Mindlessly, at the register, I pressed the suction cup ball against the glass tube. I may have pushed a little bit too hard, and to my horror, it started moving. I tried to save it, but no such luck. It came crashing down to the floor right behind the register. The checkout lady had to jump out of the way, almost killed by a tube of dark chocolate almond nut clusters. My dreams of culinary ecstasy quickly shattered to the ground, but man, did they all smell good.

Those in the store froze, and so did I—paralyzed by the impact of my actions. One tube was bad enough, but the problem was that it didn't stop there. The glass tubes crumbled one by one, crashing down to the ground in an expensive explosion of gourmet chocolate goods like a stack of perfectly toppled Dominoes. As the sugar dust settled in the quiet moment after the devastation was done, the checkout girl was speechless and horrified. Mom and I got the giggles (unfortunately). Dad quickly offered to pay the store, but the manager just screamed, "Get out!" Candy Kitchen, if you're reading this, I'm sorry. Please forgive me.

As horrible as that experience was, it revealed a powerful truth that has guided me since: Too much force, and it all falls apart. Left unchecked, the trigger in our stride can cause us to apply too much force to the world. Jesus very clearly wants us to influence the world, but *how* we do it matters. Forcing our impact on the world is not His intent.

HOLY MOTIVATIONS, UNHOLY ACTIONS

Here's why triggers are so tricky. They always begin with a holy motivation. "Righteous anger" has a dangerous side. When our anger is righteous, it's often easy to justify responses that are *not*. It becomes easy to justify using force, which takes one of two destructive patterns: controlling or revengeful actions.

Holy Motivation + Controlling Actions = Spiritual Manipulation (Forced Evangelism)

Holy Motivation + Revengeful Actions = Spiritual Violence (The Crusades or even Jihad)

Jesus calls us to something better. Let's explore this deeper.

First, let's look at controlling actions. When we try to influence the world, we try to force the world to comply with Christian morality. Let me be clear: Finding your stride does *not* mean forcing the world to comply with a Christian moral code from a position of power. When we do this, we become the religious police rather than a hope-filled movement. Even Jesus (who could have) didn't confront from a position of power. He approached the broken with gentleness and service instead of pomp and ego. Remember the woman caught in adultery? John 8: 4–11 recounts the passage:

> "Teacher," they said to Jesus, "This woman was caught in the act of adultery. The law of Moses says to stone her. What do you say?"

> They were trying to trap him into saying something they could use against him, but Jesus stooped down and wrote in the dust with his finger.

Many sermons and articles have discussed what he was writing in the dirt. I don't have an answer for that—maybe he left out that detail intentionally. What strikes me is that He knelt. He physically put himself in a posture where he did not have control. He rid himself of power. Jesus didn't force compliance; He wasn't towering over those he was trying to correct. Instead, he lowered himself. Kneeling brings us closer to the dirt. It's impossible to stay squeaky clean while kneeling. Jesus put himself in a position of surrender and submission.

Surrender to what? He wasn't surrendering to the opinions of the crowd. He wasn't submitting to the rules of the law. It's clearly something greater. I believe he was submitting His will in favor of the Father's. Maybe it was a physical representation of the words he'd become so famous for later, "Not my will but yours be done." In a moment like this, when everything in Him probably wanted to confront, fight, and defend, He chose to submit His will to a greater will. Maybe He was modeling for us what to do when our reputations are on the line, when we're in conflict, and when everything in us wants to lash out in anger.

Christians have always viewed the world as broken or in need of help. I once heard leadership expert John Maxwell explain, "If we see people as broken, we'll try to fix them. If we see them as hurt, we'll try to help them. But if we see them as valuable, we'll try to serve them." Jesus recognized the value of this woman who was being condemned on all sides—all sides, that is, but His.

When God calls us to step out with courage, it's usually an invitation to greater submission, surrender, and service—not greater control. Through the lens of Jesus, courage rarely looked like taking a stand; it often looked like taking a knee. The more we try to control the actions of the world, the more manipulative we become. Jesus was never manipulative; we shouldn't be, either.

The second unhealthy response is vengeful actions. I recognize this pattern in myself, and maybe you do, too. We see all that's broken in our world and crave justice and revenge. We take that thirst for revenge into our hands. We want to see the "bad guys" get what they deserve, don't we?

I have a friend who leads an anti-trafficking coalition, but before that, he was directly involved in arresting and prosecuting traffickers all over the world. This guy has stories like no one else. When I read his resume before meeting him, I envisioned an action movie character: someone fueled by rage with massive muscles and a deep burden for justice to make the bad guys pay. Imagine my surprise when I met him, and his gentle smile and contagious laugh caught my attention. (His muscles were decent but not huge.)

We spent a week together overseas, and he shared his stories with me. There was one thing that came through in every story: He never painted the "bad guys" as "bad guys." Instead, he saw the complexities of souls in anguish. He saw the pain in the broken ones. He wasn't fueled by rage; he was fueled by redemption. I began to see the complexities when he explained that most trafficking perpetrators have been abuse victims themselves first. Drawing out their stories, and listening to them with intentionality, he illustrated how justice and mercy can hold together. Even traffickers are created in the image of God.

One of the things that struck me from his stories is that proximity is transformational. From a distance, it's easy to conclude we're fighting the individual; it's easy for us to crave revenge. However, when we move closer, we recognize the humanity in those we're confronting and realize we're fighting against the brokenness, not the individual. That makes all the difference. We start to crave redemption instead of revenge. I think Jesus knew this, too. When he wandered the streets of Jerusalem and met tax collectors and Pharisees, he had this curious habit of joining them for dinner. What a thing—maybe Jesus knew that proximity is the key to life change.

I've always been drawn to Psalm 23:5: "You prepare a table before me in the presence of my enemies." I've envisioned that glorious day when I'll finally be honored, and my enemies will have to watch me feast at a table set up by the King of the Universe while they beg for the scraps. But what if I've missed the point? What if the table is more than just a one-seater? What does it look like for me to invite my enemies to the table? We're invited to a table in front of our enemies *to* invite them to the table, too. If our courageous response to our triggers moves us further away from those who have wounded us—instead of closer to them—maybe it's not God directing our strategy.

Scripture gives us many interesting examples of these two patterns in practice. Take Moses, for example. He grew up living in privilege after Pharoah's family adopted him. He lived in the Egyptian royal palace while his people were living in bondage and slavery. He was overwhelmed by the injustice around him and knew it wasn't right. Have you ever been there—so completely overwhelmed by the pain and suffering around you that you must do *something?*

That's a holy feeling; that's the trigger. God wants our hearts to break for the things that break His. The problem was in *how* Moses went about addressing injustice. Moses killed an Egyptian. It's the perfect example of what forceful impact looks like. Holy motivation (defending the oppressed) combined with a *controlling action* (I'll get them to stop by killing them). The exact same thing happens today. We see the brokenness in the culture around us, and it's far too easy to lash out in anger with a controlling action. We might not choose murder, but perhaps a social media meme or a petition we join to shame those making decisions we disagree with, all to control the actions of others. I don't think Jesus ever wanted his followers to control the world around them.

Hundreds of years later, Peter did something similar in the garden with Jesus. When the soldiers came to arrest Christ, Peter (overcome with the emotion of defending his friend) grabbed his sword and sliced off the ear of a soldier (punishing the soldier by bringing him pain). He had holy motivation (looking out for his friend) but took a vengeful action. That's where things went south. We have to do better. Jesus calls us to maturity, even in our response to emotional triggers.

The sad reality is that when an emotional trigger is acted upon in an unhealthy manner, the problem we create is often bigger than the very problem we set out to solve. Allow me to illustrate.

My friend Matt is building his own house. He's not having it built; he's *building* it, personally. He bought land down in Texas, bought some livestock, and then literally bought a book on how to build a house—in that order. It has to be the most Texas thing ever done. He poured the foundation, nailed down the studs, installed the plumbing, and tacked up the drywall. It's incredible. Inspired by his can-do attitude, I told my beautiful bride that I'd hang a shelf in our laundry room.

Two hours later, the shelf was still on the floor. I used a screwdriver to put a screw into the drywall, pushed too hard, and sent it right through the wall. I ended up with a big hole in the wall. Worse yet, I sent it straight into the water line for the washing machine. Water gushed through and out of the wall.

I reflected on my actions as I called a plumber—and a drywall expert—and went out to Home Depot to buy some paint. As a result of my actions, the drywall guy had to take out a bigger section of the wall to remove the damage I created.

A lot of forceful impact has been done in our world in the name of defending God. Unfortunately, it's created a bigger problem. I've often muddied the picture of Jesus by adding my controlling actions on top. Churches have unintentionally often given the message, "Get yourself cleaned up, then come to our church." The unfortunate result is that Jesus now feels out of reach for many in our society because of the controlling actions of Christians acting in His defense. The garden of Gethsemane teaches us that Jesus doesn't need our defense. My laundry room wall teaches us that when we try to force impact, chances are good that the problem we'll create is bigger than the very problem we tried to solve.

Contrast these examples with the approach we see modeled in 1st Samuel 14. Jonathan and his armor-bearer were at the base of a cliff with the rest of their Israelite warriors, and at the top of the cliff were the Philistines. This was a worst-case scenario for the Israelites, and everyone was panicking (including King Saul). They were emotionally invested in this battle, and everyone knew their lives were in danger. This is an emotionally charged, heated moment. In the middle of the night, Jonathan wakes up his armor-bearer and suggests that they climb the mountain and show themselves to the Philistines. At the surface, this might look like taking matters into their own hands and forcing it. I'm convinced it's something different. Jonathan says, "*Perhaps* the Lord will act on our behalf."

Jonathan and his armor-bearer model a better approach for us and pave the way for healthy influence in the world. They respond to an emotional trigger with a *holy motivation* and a *surrendered action*. They commit to doing something but actively surrender each of their steps to Him. A surrendered action invites God into the action. A surrendered action is taking a step and saying, "God, redirect me if this isn't what you want done." What a different world we would have if all our steps were surrendered actions instead of controlling actions.

The greatest challenge we have in choosing a surrendered action rather than a controlling or vengeful action is patience. Controlling actions and vengeful actions are both immediate— immediate action, immediate result. Meanwhile, acting with surrender is often far slower. It's a step at a time. Sometimes, it looks like a forty-year journey through the desert, taking one forward step at a time toward redemption but not experiencing it yet. Sometimes, it looks like crying with traffickers over their brokenness and facilitating justice while begging God for redemption. It requires great patience waiting for Him to make all things right. There's something magical that happens when we are faithful in the pursuit of redemption. Where are you waiting for Him to make all things right?

BACK TO GREECE

Years after the Candy Kitchen incident, I still think about that place. I can remember the details of the day and the absolute horror when it all came crashing down. Just to ensure I never forget, I carry a suction cup ball in my backpack now. I also have one on my desk. Admittedly, it's weird, and I get some stares when they fall out of my bag at the TSA desk. However, it's a perfect reminder that when I try to respond to emotional triggers with force, it all falls apart. I actually took a suction cup ball with me on a return trip to Greece not too long ago.

I was visiting my friend Sahar, who works with refugees. Her story is incredible. A former refugee herself, she escaped to Greece years ago with her life in her hands, escaping religious extremism and many threats on her life. Without any medical background, Sahar and her husband built a clinic and a church from the ground up, providing essential services for Persian refugees. She and her team have worked through all the legal hoops and licensing challenges, and the clinic is now thriving. Her work is inspirational.

Sahar is a woman who has allowed her heart to break for others, and after finding freedom for herself, she walked right back to the source of pain because her heart was broken for others. Her burden for the oppressed is clearly aligned with the heart of God. She is regularly threatened by the country she originally escaped from and by others who don't like what she's doing. Undeterred, she presses on with courage and service, knowing God will sustain her as she serves others. Each day, Sahar hears the stories of the countless masses who have endured physical and emotional trauma that no one ever should, and she's learned to vulnerably share her stories with them. Since the time she and her husband started this clinic and church, it's quickly become their entire lives. They are on call all day (and all night) long. They've learned that they can't see life change without being in proximity to the people they serve.

Sahar hasn't pushed faith on anyone. She hasn't sought to manipulate anyone's morality or make them comply with a Christian worldview. She's kept force out of the equation and walked with gentle service and love, hoping that perhaps God would act on their behalf. He has. Through her little clinic and the small Farsi-speaking church, they are experiencing a movement of hope that now extends deep within the refugee community in the camps. However, the tragic reality is still present day in and day out. Each day, new refugees arrive. Each day starts anew with stories of heartbreak and pain. The question before Sahar and before us is this: When we're craving redemption that we can't see yet, how do we sustain? To answer the question, let's return to the life raft mountain.

STACKING LIFE RAFTS

I have now returned to Greece several times and connected with hundreds of refugees there, and the image of the life-raft mountain stays in my head. When I first went to the camps, I saw it as a heaping, stinking garbage pile of broken dreams, deflated aspirations, and a depressing visual reminder that they craved redemption but hadn't reached it yet. However, I've learned to view it differently.

I'm reminded of the Israelites as they wandered through the desert. They had experienced rescue but hadn't experienced the redemption they were craving. Stuck living in the land between, they wandered aimlessly in the place between oppression and the Promised Land. Many of us live in this place, too. When our hearts break for the needs in our world (if our response is healthy), we'll find ourselves yearning for redemption, and it's so easy to feel disheartened when we realize it's not coming quickly enough. Our guts ache with desperation for the Almighty to make it right and right *now*. "How long, oh, Lord?" our hearts cry, like the Psalmist.

As they wandered through the desert, the Israelites developed a practice that I believe we can embrace, too. They stacked stones. Every time they saw the hand of God intervene in their circumstances, they'd stack stones. It didn't matter how small of an intervention or how small of a stone stack they stacked. These small stone piles became reminders when they felt like they were not arriving in The Promised Land soon enough, when redemption wasn't coming fast enough, and when they felt stuck and brokenhearted. Stone stacks were their reminder that the God who had worked before would work again. Stacking stones gave them enough courage and confidence to sustain their next forward step.

What if the life-raft mountain wasn't just a peak of deflated aspirations but a mountain of remembrance? As they awaited running forward into redemption, the refugees needed something to sustain themselves. As we await running forward into our stride, we also need something to sustain. Rescued but not redeemed—yet. What if the stack of life rafts is the fuel that keeps them sustained in this land in between? What if it can do the same for us?

SECTION 3

RELEASE

5

THE TRAP OF SHAME

I used to drag shame with me everywhere. Now, I travel light.

Travel is a regular occurrence in my work, advocating for humanitarian projects all throughout the world. My luggage almost always makes it where I'm going, except one time when it most certainly did not.

I was boarding my plane in Los Angeles on my way back to Colorado along with about a couple hundred other passengers, finding our seats and stowing our carry-ons in the overhead bins. I placed mine in the bin, and just as I did, there was a tremendous bang, and the whole plane shook violently. People lost their balance and screamed and went running for the exits. The plane wasn't even disconnected from the jet bridge; had we really just been in a plane crash? The flight attendants panicked, running to figure out what was going on. People ran for the exits while others were texting their loved ones goodbye.

As I looked out the window, the reason quickly became apparent. A luggage cart had slammed violently into the wing of the airplane. The poor guy who was driving the cart just looked down and buried his face in his hands, humiliated and defeated by his mindless mistake. The cart tore a huge hole in the wing, and the plane was clearly damaged beyond repair. This was a very expensive mistake, likely costing hundreds of thousands, if not more, to fix. Baggage literally derailed our progress.

As we all slowly calmed down, gathered our carry-on bags once again, and grumpily got off the plane, everyone stood in the terminal, taking pictures of the plane to post on social media while awaiting the assignment to a new flight. Watching the chaos around me, I couldn't help but think about the analogy: *Often, the baggage we carry with us derails our forward progress.*

Each of us carries things that hold us back from moving forward. These traps not only hold us back but also limit our capacity for the future. The sad reality is that our baggage often derails our forward progress in any number of shame-inducing, violent explosions. While there may not be a picture-taking audience documenting the whole thing on social media, it's almost always costly. We need to find a way to release our baggage so we can run unhindered into the good works for which He's designed us.

Have you ever noticed how light Jesus traveled? It's hard to imagine Him lugging around a big suitcase or pulling a rolling cart behind Him as He moved from village to village. When He sent the disciples out in Luke 9, He told them, "Take nothing with you for the trip. No walking stick, no beggars bag, no food, no money, not even an extra shirt." It is not because those things are inherently bad or because there's anything wrong with pre-planning but because Jesus knows how impactful we can be without things weighing us down.

This section is all about releasing the baggage we carry that weighs us down, and this chapter specifically focuses on the first source of our baggage: our shame. To start, we need to clarify a bit deeper. Our mistakes aren't our baggage. We've all made mistakes. It's a normal part of our human experience, and mistakes are unavoidable. It's when our mistakes begin talking to us, and we begin internalizing those messages and allowing them to shape our identity; now, we're talking about the shame that we must release. Shame works to make us believe that we are flawed, permanently broken, useless, and unworthy of the calling set before us. We all have wounds, but when those wounds make claims on our identity, they become baggage we need to release.

Over the last two decades of coaching individuals, I've repeatedly seen shame keep people from finding their stride. They've been stuck and unable to make decisions about their future direction because of the messages they've internalized from the brokenness of their past. Shame has robbed the influence and fulfillment from their future, and if we aren't intentional, it will do the same for us. If we want to move forward, we must deal with the problem of shame.

Earlier in this book, we talked about the beneficial side of painful experiences; they're a valuable tool to be used. However, often, the wounding we carry from those experiences weighs us down. Jesus invites us to release everything because when we do, it makes us *available* to receive from others and from Him. When our hands are so full of our baggage that we can't receive from Him, we've officially derailed our forward progress. It's paralyzing.

My friend Eric has taught me so much about how to release the baggage we carry. In our first meeting, he sat quietly, yet his presence carried tremendous wisdom and experience. I knew he had much to offer. As a counselor, Ph.D., pastor, and author, his expertise is tremendous, but his credibility comes not from his accolades but from his brokenness. Let me explain.

For most of Eric's young adult life, he's battled a long, personal fight with addiction. Eric's perseverance and recovery program experiences gave him a passion to help others find the same. Now, Eric is a trauma and human sexuality professor, counselor, internationally recognized speaker, and author. His work in addiction recovery has transformed the lives of thousands, and it's because he has been vulnerable and transparent with his story.

Though their stories of struggle and brokenness are completely different, Eric's message became his message, but like Rahab in the Bible. As a prostitute, Rahab lived in the city of Jericho, and Israelite spies found that her home would be their way into the city without drawing attention—*because strange men frequently visited her home at night.* She sold herself for money to anyone who would pay—certainly not the type of person we'd normally think of as an asset for God's purposes. Yet God redeemed the brokenness of her story for His purposes. Rahab hid the Israelite spies when they went on a reconnaissance trip into the city. When the enemies came looking for them, she helped the Israelites escape.

Have you ever noticed how when we're ashamed of something, we shirk back when we meet others—particularly faith leaders—because we want to hide? As a leader of a faith-based organization with Bible verses tattooed on my arms, telling people what I do for a living is always interesting. Not long ago, I met an individual for the first time at a park. I asked him what he did for a living, and he explained he worked driving trucks. Then, he asked me about my career, and at the same time, he happened to catch a glimpse of my tattoos. I told him about my career, and immediately, his posture changed. His entire demeanor changed; he was far more cautious with his words and felt the need to "clean up his act."

We all do this. When we have brokenness, and we meet someone religious, we tend to do anything we can to cover the brokenness. Shame sets in, and we hide. This is the thing that keeps so many of us from embracing the good works God has designed us for. We never find our stride in the world if we keep shrinking back and avoiding anything that may expose our brokenness to the world.

Contrast this approach with Rahab, who, despite having much to be ashamed of, invited these men of God into her home. She quickly recognized that these were Israelites, God's chosen people, and that they were on a mission directly from Him. Read Joshua 2: 8–11:

> Before the spies lay down for the night, she went up on the roof and said to them, "I know that the Lord has given you this land and that a great fear of you has fallen on us so that all who live in this country are melting in fear because of you. We have heard how the Lord dried up the water of the Red Sea for you when you came out of Egypt and what you did to Sihon and Og, the two kings of the Amorites east of the Jordan, whom you completely destroyed. When we heard of it, our hearts melted in fear, and everyone's courage failed because of you, for the Lord your God is God in heaven above and earth below.

Rahab was keenly aware that something supernatural was happening. It's intriguing that instead of closing the door and hiding (acting from the posture of shame), she welcomed them with hospitality and brainstormed a plan for their escape (the posture of openness).

Shame usually makes us shrink down. However, Rahab saw a strategic opportunity to be a part of what God was doing. It can become incredibly strategic when we dare to be honest about the brokenness of our past. Here's the key: We need to offer our brokenness to be used. We need to throw it down. Allow Rahab to illustrate. Joshua 2:15 continues with the story, "She let them down by a rope through the window, for the house she lived in was part of the city wall. She said to them, 'Go to the hills so the pursuers will not find you. Hide yourselves there three days until they return, and then go on your way.'"

The Israelites escaped by climbing down a rope. Fascinatingly, the Hebrew word used for rope can also refer to pain or suffering. I don't think that's an accident; the hanging rope is a beautiful analogy. Hung in full view of the public, anyone could see her painful brokenness. So, what do you do with the suffering and pain of your shameful past? Throw it down, chuck it out the window? Lay it down as an offering. When you do, it might just be seen by others, but it also might become the bridge to freedom for someone who needs it.

Offering our brokenness to God for His purposes is the path by which we release the baggage of shame. In it, the brokenness we carry can be transformed to serve as a bridge to freedom for others. What would it look like for you to offer your brokenness to the Lord for his purposes? Somehow, in the offering, the shame is released.

THE PURPOSE OF BROKENNESS

There are two ways our brokenness is important strategically. First, brokenness impacts our *position*. It's shocking how many scriptural heroes experienced shameful brokenness in their stories. Brokenness keeps us from leading with power and positions us as co-journeyers with others who are walking the same journey. It's almost as though it's a prerequisite for influence. What if it's precisely *because* of their past that Biblical heroes were often so effective in their work? In the eyes of God, our brokenness gives us *credibility* for our future. Paul, with his background as a murderer and persecutor of

Christians, had arguably the greatest impact of any individual in the history of our faith.

Second, when we embrace our brokenness, it impacts our *posture* toward the world. Perfection keeps us from compassion because the key to compassion is empathy. When we see our brokenness in the brokenness of others, we can show compassion. One of my friends in Colorado is a senior leader in the pro-life space. He's a strong voice for the sanctity of human life and regularly influences the government, non-profit, and faith-based sectors. He shared his story with me.

Very early in his twenties, he was engaged to a woman who became his wife. They were both in professional ministry, working at a church. They made some mistakes and, ultimately, got pregnant before marriage. For pastors, this can have huge consequences on their careers. My friend told me that he and his fiancé contemplated "making all their problems go away" with a short visit to the local abortion clinic. They didn't and, instead, chose to walk through the journey as young parents and wrestle through the shame of their actions.

Here's what struck me: This leader can look at people with compassion now because he's *been there, too.* He knows what it's like to have a baby on the way and feel like there are no options. He knows what it's like to be terrified. He doesn't lash out in anger at those who have chosen abortions. Instead, he looks upon them with compassion. He sees great value in providing care for those who have made that decision and now must live with the guilt of their actions. When we acknowledge the brokenness in our past and release the shame around it, our voice toward others changes from condemnation to compassion.

Embracing our brokenness affects our position and posture, allowing us to have both credibility and compassion in our work serving the world. If we want to find our stride, we need to tap into the brokenness in our story.

When I coach people through the process of finding their stride, I encourage them to take an inventory. Where has brokenness shown up in your past? What mistakes and short-comings have plagued your story? We can expect that God wants to use even these things for His sake. The missteps you've made have the potential to become tools to help others find hope and healing.

Shame is a powerful thing. Most of us are living below our potential not because we aren't capable but because of the shame suitcases we carry with us. Shame is that voice in the back of our minds screaming at us that we can't have the impact we feel called to because of all we've done in the past. Shame is the excess weight baggage that comes at an additional cost, gets on the baggage truck, collides with the plane, and keeps us from our destination. Shame is not God's intent for us. Shame must be released.

To release shame, we need a mindset shift. We need to understand that the things we're ashamed of can become a bridge to help lift others out of the hell they may be walking through. From a human perspective, shameful components of our story are harmful and distract from the narrative but not from God's perspective. The great task before us is to trust that God can and will bring good from even the things we're ashamed of. What brokenness in your past might become a bridge to rescue others?

RETURNING TO ERIC

Eric realized that God wanted to use his addiction background as the launching pad for influencing others. He decided to start a recovery focused church. It soon grew to 40 people and needed a weekday space to meet for recovery meetings, not just Sunday morning services. So he started looking for room to rent – but few would allow this group to meet on their church campus. Eventually, Eric heard about a church in town that was struggling. An old church with a great history, but the community had changed significantly, and they were a bit out of touch. The community had changed, drug use had climbed, the homeless population had grown substantially, and the church had sadly grown in its irrelevance. It was the perfect place for Eric's recovery program.

Nervous but determined, Eric scheduled a meeting to talk with the pastor and elders of the church about devoting a room to Eric's recovery ministry. The meeting felt incredibly intimidating from the start. He explained his story and his vision for creating a place for those on the margins, and he explained his need—one room, a few nights per week, to host a recovery ministry. There were cold stares and little movement. Eric was pretty sure he had blown the opportunity.

He got a call from the church a week later. Eric had already moved on in his mind to other places. The pastor on the other side of the phone said, "Eric, we're not going to give you a room for the recovery ministries."

"Oh, I underst—"

"... Instead, we're going to give you our church."

The leaders of the church had talked, prayed, and caught the vision of what could be—the whole church becoming a faith-based recovery center and a life-giving church again for a rapidly changing community. Lives could be changed daily. It could be a food kitchen, job training center, and rehab center, all in one. The facility was worth millions—just given to Eric and his small crew of volunteers.

Eric never had a big master plan for building a huge organization. His journey was simple. He took a step of obedience in aligning the brokenness of his life experiences (even the shameful ones) with the things God cares about, and then, God did the rest. When we take a step of obedience, God often throws gasoline on it and blesses our efforts profoundly.

The center now includes a café feeding two hundred homeless people weekly. It also includes numerous faith based and traditional recovery groups, shower stations for the poor in the community, haircuts for the poor, and so much more. The life change they have seen is tremendous, and they've become a beacon of hope in our city.

YOUR CHURCH SMELLS

Eric told me about a woman who had a radical recovery and faith conversation at his church. Having participated in and watched hundreds of lives transformed through the ministry, very few stories surprise him anymore. This encounter not only surprised him, but transformed him.

She requested an appointment to ask him questions about faith and culture. He used the opportunity to ask her about what catalyzed her transformation. Deep down, he expected her answer to be the quality of the music or the quality of his teaching on Sundays. He even would have been fine with hearing about the quality of their recovery programs or, worst case, the free lunches they offered.

"The smell," she told him.

"Umm, can you elaborate?"

"I walked in and started panicking because I wasn't ready for this."

Walking through the front doors of a church was not something she ever would have predicted for herself. It felt like an out-of-body experience, but she was desperate. She was out of other options and at the end of her rope. "So, I ran to the bathroom to escape and gather my wits, and when I got in, there was a girl hungover and vomiting in the bathroom."

She continued, "I left the bathroom and walked through the lobby, and another person smelled like booze."

Eric was speechless. He didn't know how to respond. Equal parts offended and inspired by his reeking church lobby, he wondered where this was going.

There was a long pause until she finally broke the silence. "This place smelled like my life, and I knew I would be safe. I knew I could belong here."

I am not advocating for Christian drug use or anything of the sort. The longer we walk with Him, the more we should look like Him, but hear this: Life change is often not an overnight change. Jesus extends his invitation to life for those struggling with all manner of addictions, pain, and suffering.

I can guarantee that the girl puking in the bathroom was ashamed of the fact that she was hungover at church. I'm sure the people using drugs or getting drunk the night before probably felt unqualified for the journey of being a disciple. Little did they know that God was using *even their brokenness* for the sake of His purposes.

Many of us strive to conceal our mistakes, fearing judgment and rejection. However, the truth is that the very things you feel most ashamed of might be what God uses to guide someone else to redemption. By embracing our flaws and sharing our stories, we reveal the transformative power of Jesus, showing the world that His grace is available to everyone.

6

THE TRAP OF IMAGE

I used to cling to image. Now, I embrace vulnerability.

My friend Tim is a hero. He and his wife know what it means to suffer, thrive, and be resilient. Tim taught me about refugees and how they are heroes and way-makers—heroes we need to learn from. I feel honored to know Tim.

In June 2014, he and his wife, Sarah, moved from their home in New York City to Iraq. The day they arrived was the day ISIS invaded. They thought they would serve as missionaries; they didn't realize it was a rescue mission. They had the option to turn back, but they didn't. They struggled with the fact that they had the option to escape, while those they were surrounded by could not, so they decided to stay through it and tough it out. Tim is a man of courage, and I love him for that. They had brought their three young kids with them to Iraq, and it was complete mayhem. Suffering, pain, and struggle were everywhere they looked, but while there, they helped start a school for refugee children who had fled ISIS. They remained there for over three years, and during that time, they saw the resilience and perseverance of the refugees and the Kurdish people. It permanently changed Tim's outlook on life.

Tim and I have since become very close friends, and we're always cooking up crazy ideas, which is why it didn't surprise me when he called one day with a proposition.

"Hey, mate!" (He lives in Australia, comes by it naturally.) "You want to go to Israel and Palestine with me?"

"Well, yes, yes, I do."

The trip was planned right then and there.

We recruited a few others to join us a few months later, and we headed out. We were traveling there to learn from Israelis and Palestinians. We wanted to understand the dynamics at play in the age-old conflict and witness how those dynamics resulted in horrible conditions for the vulnerable. The goal was to help start a school for Palestinian children, but we wanted to learn more before we did.

Everyone on the team preferred different airlines, so we were all flying independently. I flew through NYC and took an overnight flight straight to Tel Aviv. It was the week before Easter and Passover, and was also in the middle of Ramadan. The plane was filled to the brim. Christians, Jews, Muslims—everyone was headed to the Holy City for a pilgrimage. The plane was jam-packed; every seat was taken. It was also emotionally and religiously charged, as it was full of pilgrims whose religions had been at war with one another for centuries.

Mealtime was wild. My mind drifted to the verse about having a table set before me in the presence of my enemies. We all dined on airplane chicken or fish, the religious and cultural walls between us mightier than the seat back tray tables and noise-canceling headphones. Some bowed silently in prayer over their meals; many stood and prayed out loud, bobbing their bodies back and forth as they prayed, utilizing every corner of the plane to do so. Each population connected uniquely with the deity they worshipped. This 747 was a miniature version of Jerusalem herself—three distinct people groups, all in conflict with each other, existing in a tiny, highly pressurized, confined space. With abundant differences, one thing unified us: the masks over our faces, as this was during the height of the pandemic. Everyone's identity was thinly veiled by the fabric covering their faces.

I sat in the exit row. As it got late into the evening, the man to my left was still working on his computer as I, and all the others, were trying to doze. Eventually, he stood up to put his computer away. He clearly wasn't feeling the mask and took it off. It was a passive protest that raised just a few eyebrows, but he quickly made it clear that he was not one for the rules of societal convention. He then took his suitcase down from the bin above and proceeded to take off his pants.

Yes, he took off his pants. Right then and there. On the plane. Unmasked and standing in his underwear, he neatly folded his pants to put them back into his suitcase as he prepared himself for bed.

I have so many questions for the unmasked, pants-less man, but I'm struck by his courage. It takes tremendous courage to drop the mask—and the pants—and be vulnerable, particularly in a conflict zone. In the face of challenge, conflict, or aggression, it's easy to put on a front and hide behind our masks. We all do this, don't we? In fact, we're addicted to the masks we wear. We're addicted to our ability to appear put together, to our professionalism, our cultural norms, and our image.

We pretend we have it all together and everything is exactly as it should be in our lives. We adhere to certain cultural norms, desperate to fit in. We cling to the images we create for safety at all costs. The problem is that when we're navigating a transition or trying to discern the next steps, it's nearly impossible if we're wearing a mask.

Recently, I connected with a business leader who has been highly successful in his career. He came to me and asked for coaching; he said he was at a crossroads and didn't know what to do. Transition is always a time of insecurity and confusion, and for most of us, when we feel insecure, our default strategy is to put a mask on. This practice is highly destructive when we are attempting to find our stride to navigate our next steps. We decide to emphasize our importance to project confidence and feel more secure. His willingness to take the mask off and ask for coaching inspired me. It's a privilege to know him.

Often, the image we cling to falls short of God's intent because what He is after (and, by the way, what the world needs) is our vulnerability. The courage we're called to is the hard work of dropping our masks, dropping the image, dropping the appearances, and embracing vulnerability to allow our true selves to be seen.

UNDERSTANDING COURAGE

We are commanded to walk with courage, yet most of us have a skewed picture of what this looks like. I used to think this meant bravely walking into the world with power, pomp, and authority. I envisioned the courageous telling the world all that they're doing wrong and not being afraid of the repercussions. Many of us still operate from that same perspective. We envision warriors marching off to battle with their chests puffed out and their weapons raised high. In fact, Christians are notorious for this. Somehow, we've twisted *courage* to make it look like *correction*. As a result, we've given the impression in culture that the Church is more about what it stands *against* rather than what it stands *for*. We need to understand courage through the eyes of scripture instead.

Have you ever noticed that the command to courage is almost always coupled with a task that demands vulnerability?

In scripture, vulnerability is consistently one of the first requests from God for most of our Biblical heroes. Moses was specifically commanded to return to the city where he grew up—where everyone knew his shortcomings, where he was a known convict, where he was hated—and lead an emancipation. This required tremendous vulnerability.

In 1 Samuel 14, God gave Jonathan and his armor bearer the vision to "expose themselves to the enemy." This required incredible vulnerability. (I suppose the pants-less guy on the airplane probably had received a similar word.)

Everyone God uses, he calls to courageous vulnerability—even Mary. She was given a task that demanded greater vulnerability than any other: carrying and delivering the Savior of the world in a barn without a team of doctors, just an audience of goats and sheep. She was terrified, and the angels instructed her, "Do not fear." The courage asked of her was ultimately the courage to be vulnerable.

Most of us aspire to courage, but we don't naturally tend to associate it with vulnerability. We associate courage with bravery, strength, power, and authority. However, courage doesn't happen because we try hard or because we muster up our own strength. Scripture lays out a formula for how courage appears in Joshua 1:9: "Be strong and courageous, do not be discouraged, do not be dismayed, for the Lord your God is with you wherever you go."

Did you catch that? It's subtle but so important. The courage to be vulnerable directly results from understanding His *presence with us.* It is not something that we can generate on our own. Courage through companionship means we are dependent on God for all we do. We (American Christians) are fiercely independent, and it's to our disadvantage. The God of the Universe wants to commune with us. The natural byproduct of that communion is courage—but it comes through the vulnerability of acknowledging our dependence on Him. Is it possible that your independence has kept you from vulnerability? Is your inability to move forward possibly tied to your unwillingness to be vulnerable and dependent upon God?

In each of these scriptural examples, when an angel commands the person not to fear, it's followed up with a promise: *The Lord will be with you.* Human eyes try to muster up courage and strength. Jesus offers us something far greater—His presence—and that companionship naturally gives us the courage to face tomorrow with vulnerability.

Where do you sense God is encouraging you to drop your addiction to the masks and step into greater vulnerability? Finding our stride in the world is incompatible with the pretenses we keep. They simply cannot exist together. When we allow our image to become the priority, we slip into insecurity, comparison, and inauthenticity, and it results in a shallow life. We become pretenders. We obsess over Instagram likes and get anxious about our reputations. Have you ever noticed the level of peace people have when they remove the image mask? Often, they describe it as "a weight off their shoulders," or they'll express, "I love that we can just be ourselves with each other."

When we reach the place where we finally have the courage to be vulnerable, we need to break through the images we present to get to the core of who He created us to be, and it will bring us peace. Then, and only then, can we be used.

BACK TO JERUSALEM

While in Israel, we had the tremendous privilege of staying at the King David Hotel. If you're unfamiliar, the King David is one of Jerusalem's oldest and most elaborate hotels. Well outside of our price range, the accommodations were a gift from someone else. As I entered the sprawling marble lobby, I got more than a few looks from the tuxedoed bellmen. Maybe the ripped-up jeans and flip-flops I was wearing weren't the usual attire of the world's elite.

One thing that struck me as odd was that the floor appeared to have graffiti all over it. Curious, I went over to investigate. It turns out that it was signatures from previous guests—Barack Obama and Bono, and the list went on and on. With each step, I felt the pressure to have my act together. "Best behavior," as my parents used to say before we walked into someone's nice home for dinner.

Here's the thing: I don't think any of the celebrities *asked* for a Sharpie to mark up the floor. They were asked to by the hotel. Here's the truth that makes vulnerability so much more challenging: The world worships the masks we wear. The "put-together self" gets praise from the world, which makes it far harder to reveal the true self. Yet the true self is what's required to serve the world.

A few days later, we were on our way to Bethlehem. We helped our friends start a school in the village of Cana in the Nazareth district, and in the process, we visited some of the holy sites. Our friend Bob and his organization were the ones instigating this project. As we all piled into the tiny rental car to head out to Cana, Bob opted to get into the tiny trunk of our Jeep. Keep in mind that Bob is over six feet tall and is a multiple-time *New York Times* bestselling author. He insisted and wouldn't be moved despite our best efforts. It didn't make sense to me at all until we arrived in Bethlehem.

A couple of hours later, we were pulling up to the birthplace of Jesus. As we approached the church, the weight of what we were about to see overcame me. I was about to walk upon the site where the Divine descended and took the form of a baby. Talk about vulnerability. We serve a vulnerable God. A God who chooses vulnerability just to be *with* us. There's a door you must walk through to get into the church building that's been built on the site. It's short. I mean, it's *really* short. Every person needs to duck to get to where Jesus was born. There's something to that. Image and ego puff us up; they balloon our heads to the point that we aren't recognizable anymore. Success inflates, but Jesus isn't interested in that.

The contrast with the King David Hotel rang in my ears. The world worships our ego; the world celebrates the masks we wear. Maybe Bob knew something I was missing: There is no room for ego or a puffed-up image when visiting Jesus. Where have you been clinging to masks of image when you could be vulnerable instead?

Jesus expects that we'll lower ourselves to meet with Him. It takes great vulnerability to be used by God. If I'm going to be used by Jesus, I need to unmask and get vulnerable.

If we want to find our stride in the world, we need to release our image, and the way to do that is to embrace vulnerability. Thanks, pants-less guy, for the lesson you taught me.

7

THE TRAP OF GREAT EXPECTATIONS

I used to carry expectations like spinning plates. Now, I've started letting them fall.

My father was a pastor when I was growing up, and people always had expectations that the pastor would learn to take on new hobbies—*their* hobbies, to be exact, including dog ownership. Yes, truly, someone "gifted" us a dog once. (The thing was mean and awful. If you're thinking of buying one for your pastor as a surprise Christmas gift, please reconsider.) It was Christmas morning, and someone put a big, angry, full-size dog on our front porch, truly intended as a gift; they were there to hand it off. It had a bow around its neck. The parishioners waited with it to greet my dad, gift it to our family, and thank him for his kind shepherding of the flock. He took the dog (much to my dismay) and put it in the backyard. We had the animal for months, and my siblings and I were terrified of it. It was the size of a Pitbull and had the attitude of one, too. All it really meant was that we wouldn't go outside any longer, for fear for our lives. My dad named him "Jambo," which is Swahili for "hello." It was ironic because his temperament didn't align with a friendly greeting. Other words may have been more appropriate. Dog ownership wasn't the only weird expectation that church members had for the pastor's family; they had plenty of others.

The expectations we carry with us can easily derail us as we try to find our stride in serving the world. We'll explore three types of expectations in this chapter: the expectations others have of us, the expectations we have of ourselves, and the expectations we have of God. All three are riddled with landmines and can easily derail us as we seek to take steps toward our future.

External Expectations

The most common expectation church members had for our family was that my dad would learn to play golf. In fact, Dad had church members buying him golf clubs, purchasing his greens fees, setting appointments with golf pros, etc. There was only one problem: Dad is a notoriously horrible golfer. Everyone was convinced they could change him, yet everyone was wrong. They absolutely could not.

In one of the churches he pastored, someone decided to gift him with one of the nicest, most expensive drivers made at the time. It was a wonderful gift, though we simply didn't know what to do with it. It sat in our home for months until Dad and I finally decided we needed to test it out so we could tell the guy how well it worked. It was a beautiful New York summer evening when the sun held on as long as it possibly could before it finally surrendered to the horizon at around 9:30 p.m. We took the driver to the range and got a bucket of balls. The smell of fresh-cut grass infiltrated our nostrils. Our nervous laughter interrupted the quiet, serious expressions on the golfers' faces and the "ping" sound of balls being hit over two hundred yards down the range. We didn't belong here—clearly.

We got a lane far on the end of the range because we knew it'd be lucky if we happened to connect once or twice with the ball. Truly, we're that bad. After a few annoyingly unsatisfying swings, I decided to take out my anger and get a bit of a runup, as though that could help. I swung with all my might and made brilliant contact with the ball. Weirdly, I didn't even hit the ground. I made perfect contact—a drive for the ages. However, when I got the club above my head on the backswing, it felt much lighter than it did at the start.

The head of the club easily sailed one hundred yards past the ball. I think I'd win if you got points for shattering a titanium driver. We had to stop the driving range so I could jog out to look for the head. We were afraid the ball retriever would run over the club head, which wouldn't be good for anyone. There was no repairing Big Bertha, but she went out in a blaze of glory. Some choose to merely drop the expectations of others; apparently, I choose to shatter them entirely.

In your effort to find your stride, you'll have to deal with the expectations that others have of you—external expectations. Many of the individuals I've coached through transitional seasons have gotten stuck when dealing with the expectations of others: expectations to carry on the family business or expectations to go to law school or continue a particular educational path, etc. These expectations can paralyze people and keep them from pursuing the good works they've been made for.

To navigate through the external expectations hanging on you, the first step is to name them. Stop and consider the expectations others have placed on your life and consider whether these expectations are reasonable (i.e., you're married, and your spouse expects you to be faithful to him/her and love him/her unconditionally) or unreasonable (i.e., you're in a family and, therefore, will be a part of the family business whether you want to be or not). Then, begin to seek wisdom about how to drop these unreasonable external expectations.

We need to come to grips with disappointing others and, in some cases, setting boundaries with them. Navigating through a season of transition into a new adventure usually includes uncomfortable conversations with those who may have a different vision for your life. We must learn to be okay with disappointing others on our way toward embracing our future good works, which He's prepared for us to do.

INTERNAL EXPECTATIONS

In college, I remember joining Dad for another round of golf. This time, it was out on Coronado Island in San Diego. It's a beautiful public course with stunning views of the bay and city, beautiful weather, and tee times. We hadn't ever played a course with tee times before, and we arrived a few minutes late. The fact that there were tee times should have been our first clue that this was not for us.

When we arrived, there was already a line of people behind us. We got ready and raced off to the first hole as the crowd behind us frustratingly glared at us. As we walked up to the tee, a third person was assigned to our group. He was on the phone. It looked like maybe he had done this golf thing before, but he seemed friendly enough.

Dad bravely got up to hit the ball first. After a couple of swings, he eventually made contact—and the ball bounced its way in front of us about thirty yards. I got up there next and prayed I'd hit the ball. I did so with a lot of gusto. The only problem was it sliced hard to the right and ended up on the green... of the eighteenth hole next to us.

Then, the guy joining us got up. He was mid conversation with his spouse and still had his phone to his ear. He pinched it between his shoulder and ear and said, "Hold on, baby," then, without looking at the ball, shot it straight as an arrow two hundred yards onto the right green.

As soon as he hung up the phone with his wife, we started talking to him. We told him that we were horrible golfers and that he shouldn't hang out with us. He should play ahead. He didn't budge. We told him it would only get worse—which it did. He still didn't budge. He stayed with us as we ten-plus putted so many holes. Each hole, I'd pray my shot would go in. I'd tense up my body and stress and try with all my might to do better. However, the harder I tried, the worse it would get. The expectations I carried for myself—to be better, to not embarrass myself any further, to repair the situation, all those expectations—were missed. Dad and I both were an absolute nightmare on the course. People were waiting consistently on the hole behind us all day. Still, the guy didn't leave us.

We ended up playing all nine holes with him—despite numerous suggestions for him to "play ahead." He wanted the fellowship. We talked about life, faith, and family. Here's the thing: When we lose our expectations of ourselves and accept our limitations, we become available.

I've found that the best way to release our unhealthy internal expectations is to learn to rest in God's acceptance. Acceptance means accepting the limits we have. Many of us have warped the idea of becoming "all things to all people." We've read it as an instruction that we should be modern-day Renaissance men and women and be good at everything. That's not scriptural. We must accept, acknowledge, and adhere to our limitations, recognizing them as gifts.

In his article, *Pastors and the Gift of Limits*, author Peter Scazzero writes about the gift of limits by referring to the temptations of Christ in the desert. In the desert, the Enemy tempts Christ to turn stones into bread. Christ certainly has the power. He also has the hunger, but it wasn't the time. The rocks remain rocks. Jesus accepted the limits established by God for His role and His timing. Jesus healed many but did n[2]ot heal *all*. He accepted that there were limits to His role and His timing. He received these limits as *gifts*. What does it look like for you to receive your limitations as *gifts*, recognizing that in the weakness of your limitations, His strength is magnified?

My dad and I weren't the caliber golfers that our friend would have been hoping to spend the day with, but what if we were just what he *needed*? What if the expectations you saddle yourself with are the very things you need to drop to be available for the good works God has intended?

EXPECTATIONS OF GOD

There's one more type of expectation we carry, which we need to dive into next. Many of us carry specific expectations of God. We believe He'll act a certain way or provide us with a certain desire of our heart. Perhaps even more so when we're looking to serve the world by finding our stride. When He doesn't come through the way we planned, it creates immense disappointment. Can you relate to disappointment with God? What we do with our disappointments matters.

We were golfing in San Diego because Dad was pastoring a church there. Unfortunately, the church did not go to plan. He felt very clearly that God had called him to this pastorate, but from the moment he arrived, it was "outlast, outwit, outplay." His integrity was called into question. Every decision

---

2   Scazzero, P. (2003) *Pastors and the Gift of Limits*
     https://www.emotionallyhealthy.org/wpcontent/uploads/2013/08/
     Pastors_and_the_GIft_of_Limits_Toby.pdf

was scrutinized. There were even petitions in the church lobby to have the senior pastor impeached, and a website was set up against him. As a college kid watching my dad's career raked over the coals, I found myself struggling with anger. Smacking the golf ball (on those rare occasions I could actually hit it) felt great as a release of our anger and aggression.

All the accusations were false, but they damaged his reputation nonetheless. This was not the picture we had of what this assignment would look like at the onset. It was to be the pinnacle of his career, the largest church he'd ever pastored, as it came with immediate nationwide notoriety. The only problem was that Dad was miserable. The church was eating him alive. I couldn't just blame those who were attacking Dad—that part was easy; they were jerks. The harder dynamic was the frustration and anger we had toward God. "You told us to come here, Lord, but for *this?* You didn't even warn us! We never would have come!"

This happens to each of us, whether we're in pastoral ministry or in the for-profit world. Medical professionals, teachers, and stay-at-home parents all deal with disappointment when we have expectations of God that go unmet.

In Matthew 11, John the Baptist was in prison and struggling because his expectations weren't aligning with reality. He had high hopes for Jesus; after all, he was the one who baptized Him and saw the Holy Spirit descending like a dove and landing on Jesus. John had reached a low point in his life and was put in prison. He was angry and started to question God. The prison warden probably gave him one call to make, and he decided to call Jesus—not to ask for help but to question Him. Verse 2 says, "When John, who was in prison, heard about the deeds of the Messiah, he sent his disciples to ask him, 'Are you the one to come, or should we expect someone else?'"

I think John was really saying: "Are you *actually* the Messiah because I would think that if you were the Messiah, my circumstances would probably be different right about now?" Man, I can relate to that.

John put words to what we all have wanted to voice at one time or another. We've had high expectations of God and what our lives would look like with Him. These expectations can cripple us and load us down with prerequisites: "God, if you do *x,* then I'll serve... I'll give... I'll invest myself in the needs of the world." Many followers of Jesus get stuck right here. These expectations become toxic if left unchecked.

We need a ritual of release. We need to practice the release of these expectations so that we can gently navigate the twists and turns of our lives.

I remember more than one occasion walking with my dad and hiking through the foothills, openly processing about the season his career was in. I was angry on his behalf, but he remained gentle. I was brash; he was measured. I called down hellfire and brimstone; he prayed for blessings for those who were attacking him. However self-controlled he was, the brokenness came out through disappointment. He felt disappointed with God, thinking that what He had originally promised about this church and this new position wasn't being fulfilled. This wasn't helping his career journey; it was hurting it. His reputation was being slandered, and it had very real consequences for his future employment. Dad felt abandoned, dismissed, and disregarded.

Deep down, I think Dad felt he'd eventually be vindicated, that he'd experience redemption, and that hope would come. Sadly, it didn't. After resigning battered and beaten from the church, our family needed to heal. With no job, fresh wounds, and no capacity for a new challenge, we moved a thousand miles away from California to the pine trees, clear air, and mountains of Colorado. Dad struggled to find work, but being a fighter, he found something to sell: air purifiers.

When you're a shepherd, leader, and preacher, being reduced to selling air purifiers is hard. His disappointment was palpable. Dad was wired to care for and protect people and shepherd their souls, and now, he had to pitch a product instead. Day after day, he'd lock himself in his home office and force himself to make cold calls, swallowing his pride and requiring himself to work to provide for the family.

Air purifiers work in a beautiful way. They suck in all the dirty and harmful particles in the air through their filter, trap them, and release fresh, clean air into the room. They remove the filth, the brokenness, and the toxicity in the room.

Each day, Dad plugged away with his sales calls. He embraced the simple rhythms. He'd begin his day in the Word, rehearsing the promises God had made to Him. He rehearsed the promises made in scripture and began to realize that the things God had actually promised maybe weren't aligned with the expectations we had all placed on Him. He had expected favor yet received criticism. He had expected a platform and a promotion but was pushed out instead. He had expected to be vindicated for his faithfulness but ended up the center of swirling controversy instead.

But what if God hadn't ever promised favor, platform, promotion, or vindication?

Dad began to get to work, picking up the phone, looking up a number, and following a pre-written script. A curious thing began to happen.

"I can't talk right now. I'm in an emergency. My daughter's just been in an accident."

"I can't talk right now. I've just been diagnosed with cancer."

Dad started praying with each of the people he was calling. No platform, no pedestal. No preaching, no performance. He only needed gentleness, patience, kindness, and compassion. We saw a new side of Dad. He was not ministering from expertise but from a place of released expectations. Slowly but surely, he was releasing all the unhealthy expectations of what a platform would look like, and he came to reflect more of God's character in the process. His basic daily rhythms became an air purifier themselves, sucking up all the toxic expectations he had carried and replacing them with purity.

Releasing the unhealthy, toxic expectations we carry sometimes requires an air purifier—simple daily rhythms to suck the toxins away. Disciplined daily rhythms recentered dad. He released the toxic expectations he had of God (that God would give him a big platform and more influence on the crowds) and found himself clinging to the promises God *had actually* given—not promises of a platform but promises of daily provision, not promises of fame but promises of presence.

What toxic expectations of God do you carry? When we get disappointed because our expectations of God don't align with the reality we're experiencing, we need to find a simple task to do, simple rhythms to instill, and simple disciplines to embrace. We need to focus on the simple promises of scripture. What are the actual promises God offers for your life? To provide. To work all things for the good. To always be there. To comfort. Release the toxic expectations you have of God and embrace His promises instead. If you want to find your stride, you have to shatter the unhealthy expectations others have of you, and you need to release the expectations you carry of God.

SECTION 4

IDENTITY

8

ADOPTED HEIRS

—◈—

I used to try to make a name for myself. Now, I've taken the name of another.

Years ago, I was flying from Denver to San Diego for a work conference. It was an early morning flight, and Denver's weather is notoriously bad in the Spring. It was snowy and cold, and I was late. After parking, I ran into the airport as fast as I could and jumped into the shortest security line. I handed the security officer my license, and after an intimidating stare down, he concluded I was who I claimed to be. I grabbed my carry-on bag, jacket, phone, and keys and raced off, less than half put together. I ran to get to my gate, jumped on board a smooth flight, and looked forward to the sunshine when I landed. Upon arrival in San Diego, I headed toward the rental car station to pick up the vehicle on the reservation. When I got to the counter, the lady pulled up my reservation and asked for my credit card and ID.

"ID—wait. Where's my ID?"

I looked everywhere—pockets, bag, jacket pockets, the floor, the person in line behind me's jacket pockets, everywhere.

I just had it—back in Denver.

I tried charming the lady at the desk. It turns out that my charm strategies aren't any good. I tried bribing her, but that didn't work either. (IOUs apparently don't hold a lot of weight.)

"I'm sorry, sir. I can't help you without your ID." I was fresh off the plane in a new city, having just landed without any way to move forward. I had lost my ID somewhere between security and the plane in Denver, and now, I was a thousand miles away with no way to get a car or a return flight. I was stuck—royally stuck.

This officially counts as an identity crisis. Have you ever noticed that it's extremely hard to move forward when your identity seems lost or in question? It plagues all of us. You can't move forward very well if you don't know who you are or what you're made for. In our effort to find our stride, we must land the plane of identity if we want to move forward. We need to walk with a clear sense of identity.

Often, this identity crisis has profound repercussions. In the context of leadership in the workplace, in particular, many leaders create toxic work environments because they haven't landed on who they are or how they work when faced with challenges. An insecure identity can wreak havoc on a team, culture, relationship, family, or organization. We all want to take tangible steps forward, but it's impossible when we second guess every step because we are insecure in our identity. This section is all about embracing a distinct and secure identity.

THE COMPONENTS OF IDENTITY

When asked to introduce ourselves, most of us answer the question with a description of what we do. Yet, to find our stride in the world, we need a more convincing answer about who we are rather than just what we do. We need language to articulate a specific identity. At a very basic level, three core components shape our identity: our name, our perspectives, and our gifts. This section of the book will explore each of these components in-depth, as they carry significant implications for us. This chapter will begin with unpacking the first concept: our name.

From childhood sports to university studies to our professional careers, each of us carries one primary objective: to make a name for ourselves. We labor to stand out and shine above others. Everything we do is competition-based. If we outwork the others, we'll rise to the top. If we out-discipline the others—show up early, stay on the field late—we'll go farther and faster than those around us. We live to make a name for ourselves, and our culture has emphasized the importance of this. We introduce standardized tests in the earliest elementary grades. Competitive sports programs begin as early as age seven. We count social media likes and follows obsessively. It's made us crazy. We've tied our worth to our name, and the way to make a name is to find more followers. We strive to capture any advantage we can, all to build a sense of self-worth and importance. The problem is that striving for self-worth becomes an obsession that never ends. This striving also subversively and subconsciously makes us view others as competition, not as those deserving our love and service.

Is there any way off this hamster wheel of competition? I believe there is. Does scripture carry insights for us in this work of building a name for ourselves? I believe it does. To look at it deeper, we need to consider the spiritual concept of adoption.

Ephesians 1:5 says that long before He set the Earth's foundations, God decided to *adopt* us to His family through Jesus Christ (The Message). You and I are adopted royal heirs, and the implications of this truth are profound.

Understanding Adoption

My friend Doug is an inspiration. He and his wife were grand-parents (several times over) and in their mid-sixties when he told me about the new adventure they felt called to. Specifically, they felt God had called them to adopt two young special needs kids. He asked my advice about whether it'd be strange to have grandkids older than their kids. They worked with the court system in Oregon and eventually landed on two young kids who captured their hearts, and they moved through the adoption process.

Doug has shaped my understanding of the Gospel deeply. He understood that the good news of the Gospel is the good news of adoption, and it's changed everything. Doug identified as one who's been adopted by God and brought into His family, and as a result, he couldn't help but share that adoption with others.

Here's why this good news is so good: We are given a name in our adoption. We don't make one for ourselves. The way off the hamster wheel of competition and self-worth strategies is to take the name of another.

Doug sent me a virtual link to watch their court ceremony when they finalized the adoption. The courtroom was filled with balloons, and friends and family packed the house. The judge went through the motions of the announcements until Doug and his wife interrupted and asked to say a few words. The judge obliged, and Doug opened a paper and began to read. He and his wife, Ruth, read vows to their new children one by one. Doug was crying. His wife was crying. The judge was crying. I was a mess. It was one of the most beautiful things I've ever witnessed.

Adoption comes with perks. Yes, you receive a new name. Yes, you receive freedom from competition and striving for worth. However, it also carries additional benefits. The perks of a spiritual adoption are tremendous, starting with unrestricted and immediate access to God. The invitation of adoption is to experience God as *Father*—intimate, close. The list goes on: provision, protection, the hope of eternity, and everlasting joy. These benefits are all on the list. Additionally comes the freedom to be oneself—true and vulnerable, without any pretense.

Families can be a tricky thing. We have more than enough examples of challenging families in our world. Even the most put-together families have conflict, dynamics of shame and honor, and their fair share of secrets they'd like to keep hidden. However, at its best, a great family is one where you don't feel pressure to accomplish. You don't feel pressure to keep the family together or to perform, and you have nothing to prove. You don't *earn* a place in a family; you're *given* a place. At its best, a healthy family is a safe space—somewhere to be yourself, a community and context to do things *with*, not *for*. One of the reasons we have so much dysfunction in the Church today is that we use our gifts and strengths to accomplish *for* God rather than relishing in the fact that we are part of the *family* with nothing to earn and nothing to prove.

As we attempt to discern our next steps and navigate through seasons of transition, it's far easier if we have a firmly established sense of identity. We can love and serve others rather than compete with them for recognition and worth. When we rest in the name we've been given, we can forget about making a name for ourselves.

In the US, adoption has gotten a bad reputation. It's sometimes cruelly viewed like a second-place option and pity-driven, with the attitude, "Sorry the birth family didn't work out; let's see what we can do to scrape together something that's a good second-place option." This terribly damaging narrative is why adoptive parents work so hard to help their children realize they've been prayed for, desired, dreamt of, and *chosen*.

Likewise, our spiritual adoption is not a second-place option. It's not a backup plan for when it doesn't work on our own. Our *truest selves* are found as adoptive heirs of the King—prayed for, desired, dreamt of, chosen. The good news of our faith is not just that we've received salvation; it's that we've been placed into a family and have a new name.

Have you ever seen someone who truly knew their identity was grounded in their sonship? They don't strive but are willing to try anything because their identity doesn't hinge upon their success. Immune to the pressure to make a name for themselves, they have freedom from embarrassment, failure, and even fear itself. This is particularly important for those of us who are attempting to discern our next steps. As we work through a season of transition, a grounded identity gives us the freedom to experiment.

What would you attempt if you knew that failure didn't matter? What would you do if you knew you were just as loved if you succeeded or failed? That's the magic of an adoption to sonship—unconditional acceptance and love. To navigate your next steps, you need to operate from an understanding of your adoption.

From here, we can begin to explore our uniqueness. In the next two chapters, we'll explore the other components of our identity: our perspectives and our gifts. Both of which empower us to bring hope and love into the world.

9

PERSONALITY ARCHETYPES

I used to think I could be all things to all people. It turns out that I can't.

In early 2020, sitting on a rooftop patio with the twinkling lights of an ancient Middle Eastern city below and the warm, gentle breeze coming off the Mediterranean shores, it was easy to feel the illusion of peace. Yet I was in Southern Lebanon, and I was looking south to the northern corner of Israel on the horizon in the distance. Deep in Hezbollah territory, this was probably not the safest place for us to be. Maybe it was the jetlag keeping me up, or the signs declaring "death to America," the monuments celebrating terrorists and suicide bombers who had carried out attacks on westerners, or the fact that violent flareups tended to happen unannounced and often. Either way, my friend Jimi and I sleeplessly wondered how it was that we got here and if we'd ever get out. We took comfort in the fact that Jesus was present here—quite literally. A couple of thousand years ago, Jesus walked these very same steps.

These dusty streets were the place where the Canaanite woman begged Jesus to heal her daughter (recorded in Matthew 15). Maybe you remember the passage. She's desperate for Him to heal her daughter, and his disciples remind Him that she's a Canaanite woman and not from Israel. Jesus initially appears hesitant to heal, but she persists in her request. She's instigating, picking a fight with the established religious and cultural systems. She pushes the Almighty for healing and access to the privileges normally only allowed for the Israelites. Cultural rules and regulations insisted she had no right to access the Messiah. She was determined that the opportunity to become a royal heir was not only for the Israelites but also for everyone else. The passage records that she was rewarded for her faith and challenging the system, as her daughter received healing. Today, the Middle East is still filled with brave souls who instigate fights against cultural and religious boundaries to become heirs of the King. Jimi and I were there to meet with one such soul. His name was pastor Mo.

Mo was a large icon of a man. Originally of Palestinian descent, he had invited us to come visit and learn about his work. We met him at the airport in the capital city, then loaded into his Jeep and made the journey south into more hostile territory. When we finally reached our destination, we had been warned that the best thing to do was to get inside the building quickly and quietly. This is not a place you want to attract extra attention. I was terrified. Mo, on the other hand, had incredible confidence, strength, and peace even in the face of tremendous persecution. His life was constantly hanging in the balance, yet he was calm and at peace. I was drawn to figure out his secret: How could he be so peaceful even in the war zone around him?

Mo was living with congruence. Finding congruence is a core component of our identity and is necessary to find our stride. Congruence is the alignment between the natural *way* we engage with the world around us and the actual role in which we serve. Let's unpack this idea of congruence a bit further.

THE CONGRUENT LIFE

Our culture has been obsessed with strengths assessments, personality tests, and giftedness profiles for years. We are keenly aware that our personality, views, and perspectives shape our identity and patterns of interacting with the world. Many of us can articulate our Myers Briggs results or our Enneagram numbers on demand, but few of us have allowed these insights to have a significant voice in our careers and vocational next steps. The truth is that our unique personalities and the default ways we interact with the world deeply impact our future. If you want to find your stride, you must explore the unique disposition you carry.

In our search to bring hope into the world, I've found that there are four primary ways we interact with the world around us. These ways can be categorized through four different archetypes: the architect, the instigator, the mobilizer, and the helper. Each of these personality archetypes may face the same problem, but each will have a different way of bringing a valuable solution to that problem. Each has a different underlying motivation and path to success. Most of us have played all these roles in specific contexts, but we all have a default disposition that we resonate with most deeply. To find your most dominant archetype, consider how you operate in times of stress and rest. In times of stress and conflict, we naturally go to the disposition we feel most comfortable in. In times of rest, we do the same. We tend to default to these roles on the polar sides of the spectrum. It's the land in between where things get murky.

Each archetype can be illustrated by the Bible characters we've explored thus far in this book, so let's use them to unpack a bit deeper.

When faced with a challenge, those who have an architect perspective attempt to solve it by building structures, systems, and strategies. Highly calculated, they take in as much information as possible and formulate a well-thought-out plan. Scripturally, we see the example of Nehemiah (who we've already talked about earlier). After seeing the status of the wall around Jerusalem, he devoted himself to making a plan. He built strategies and staffed teams to rebuild the wall and bring protection again to Jerusalem. Architects see the path to success as excellent strategic thinking and operational progress. In a professional setting, a person who operates from this disposition would find the greatest satisfaction in a role focused on implementation; a good example is operations officers. In a family, this disposition may present as the one who has the calendar out and is planning the details and coordinating who's doing what and when.

Contrast this approach with those who operate from an instigator perspective. These individuals resonate more with a "cut now, measure later" perspective and are driven by a strong sense of justice. Often the first to move, they are highly aggravated by inaction; they dive in and adjust as they go. As we discussed earlier, the example here is Jonathan and his armor bearer in 1 Samuel 14. The two climbed up a cliff to attack the Philistines, and the best plan they could muster was, "Perhaps the Lord will act on our behalf!" Instigators are content with a high degree of risk and trust. Mistakes aren't viewed as failure; the only true failure in their mind is inaction. Eager for impact, these individuals come alive in forward movement. In a business setting, instigators tend to be most comfortable in entrepreneurial settings, start-ups, and maybe even investments where risk is inherent. In families, individuals wired this way may notoriously be the ones always asking the question, "Why not?"

Next, consider the mobilizer. Unwilling for anyone to be left behind, those with this perspective are adamant about getting others into the movement. The example here is John the Baptist, the voice of the one calling in the desert in Matthew 3:1–3: "In those days, John the Baptist came, preaching in the wildness of Judea and saying, 'Repent, for the kingdom of heaven has come near.'" The mobilizer perspective carries a deep burden to have others join the movement. Meaning comes through getting others involved, and success isn't actually successful if it's done alone. This perspective leads mobilizers to include others and build consensus and excitement around a cause. In a business setting, roles like recruitment, marketing, and coaching tend to be a great fit.

Last but definitely not least, we have helpers. Those who operate from this perspective dramatically prefer to support others in their pursuit of success. They ensure the right support is in place to help others thrive. Think of Rahab dropping the rope to lead others to freedom. Those with this perspective take joy in seeing others thrive and define success as seeing others accomplish great tasks. In companies, those with this disposition love serving in training, equipping, coaching, and administration roles. In families, they make sure no one is falling behind or missing out.

Each of these perspectives brings tremendous value to organizations, cultures, families, and relationships. Architects bring a plan. Instigators are catalysts for action. Mobilizers get everyone involved, and helpers ensure the success of others. Organizations need all four perspectives in their midst to ensure success. It's also easy to incorrectly assume that great leaders come from a certain archetype, but that isn't true. Each perspective carries vital leadership skills, and there are examples of incredible leaders with each of these dispositions.

Furthermore, each archetype reflects the character of Christ uniquely.

While these categories are not intended to box anyone in, they can provide helpful insights if we notice trends in our actions. As we've already mentioned, each of us has (at times) operated from each of these perspectives; however, one probably resonates with you most deeply. We tend to have one perspective that is our default, and our goal should be to find roles (career roles, volunteer roles, and relationship roles) that allow us to operate from our default perspective. When this happens, we live with great congruence. In contrast, dissonance is created if we are in a business or relationship role that requires us to operate from a perspective that is different from our natural wiring.

Most of us aspire to function in all these ways, but if we try to be all these dispositions, we end up feeling dizzy and disoriented. This is where the value of community comes in. Our organizations, churches, volunteer teams, and families need community. We are not wired to provide each of these outlooks individually. We need the perspectives of others to balance the equation. An instigator needs an architect to help formulate a plan. An architect needs a mobilizer to rally others around the cause. Without a helper, they never make progress or find freedom. The beautiful thing about the body of Christ is diversity. We need each other—not only each other's gifts but also each other's perspectives.

Back to Lebanon

A true instigator, Mo was helping Syrian refugees find hope in the Middle East. He was contagious and polarizing; everywhere he went, people either wanted to join him or they wanted to kill him. For example, he once walked into a meeting with a wealthy businessman. Within thirty minutes of his first introduction and sharing his vision, he walked out with a check for nearly a million dollars to turn his vision for a refugee hospital into a reality. On the other hand, he had also been poisoned, imprisoned, and violently assaulted—each several times. He was supremely gifted as a leader, vision caster, fundraiser, evangelist, and champion for the rights of refugees, but not everyone was happy about that.

As a child, Mo had to flee for his life under the threat of danger and attack. He was one of the lucky few to escape Lebanon. Eventually, he ended up studying and acquiring an accounting degree from an excellent school in the US. After graduation, he achieved significant success in business, but he and his wife still felt unsettled, that perhaps God was inviting them into a story bigger than themselves. They decided to leave the stability of their lives and move to Southern Lebanon to start a church and community outreach center in a war zone. The move made no logical sense. The local government wasn't happy about it. Regardless, there was no stopping Mo when he set his mind to something. The organization he was in managed to start a thriving church, refugee hospitality center, farm, camp, and job training center and did it all on a shoestring budget. They'd start and stop new initiatives all the time, throwing everything against the wall and seeing what sticks. It'd be dizzying to most, but Mo was in an organization and role that aligned well with his personality.

It wouldn't have worked by himself, but Mo was surrounded by his kids, who were brilliant in their own right. They were architects, shaping plans and strategies for each of the unique initiatives they led and volunteers they engaged. Mo's bride was a helper, providing the wisdom and empowerment to make the whole thing work. She was just as vibrant of a leader as he was, and the organization showed it.

I was inspired and a bit jealous, to be honest. As a natural mobilizer, I was working for an American organization, trying to help it grow. I was attempting to recruit volunteers and find partners and donors who could get involved. The problem I encountered was that I was working in an organization that was not ready to prioritize growth. Recruiting and engaging more people in our work was nearly impossible because of the organizational limits we had. The challenge crushed me. Because of it, I was stuck, paralyzed, and dissatisfied in my career, which felt void of meaning. There was dissonance between my natural wiring and the organization where I served. Shortly after the trip to Lebanon, I realized I needed to leave.

Mo was operating from his natural disposition. I was not. As much as my role was in congruence with my natural disposition, the organization was not. When we operate from our strengths, we experience great satisfaction and meaning. When we don't, we feel restless and stuck. Are you currently experiencing congruence or dissonance in your vocation?

10

GIFTS ON THE RUN

I used to think my gifts were intended for me. Now, I know they're intended for others.

One of the best gifts I've ever received was when I was sixteen. My first car was a 1986 Ford LTD, a gift given to my sister and me by my grandfather. He had treated it so well for many years and decided to part ways with it for us to have. If you're familiar with the car, it certainly wasn't a beauty, but it was ours. While Grandpa had taken great care of it, it had quite a few miles and was *definitely* showing its age. It'd shake and rattle when it idled, and you were never quite sure whether it'd break down or keep going.

We named her Bernie, and she quickly grew on us, even with her flaws. We loved her for what she represented. First, she reminded us that we were loved; Grandpa loved us and wanted to be kind to us. Gifts have a way of doing that. They remind us that we're thought of and that we're loved. This is true also with the gifts we receive from God. We've each received specific and unique gifts from God. There's no place for being insecure or bashful about the gifts you've received.

Pay attention to them; God has given them to you to remind you that He loves you. These gifts may include abilities, spiritual gifts, financial resources, relationships, and time.

Second, Bernie represented freedom and power. She brought us power—not literally. Literally, in fact, she had very little power. However, figuratively, she gave us plenty, and not only that, but she gave us a measure of autonomy—the ability to make some decisions about where we'd go and what we'd do. God gives gifts much in the same way. He gives us His power and authority and gives us a measure of autonomy to decide where to go and what to do. He doesn't micromanage our actions; instead, He empowers us to decide what we think is the most strategic and effective use of our gifts. God allows us a measure of autonomy in how we use the gifts and power He's given us. That autonomy is immensely freeing. If you want to try creative ways to put your gifts to work, go for it! The only command is that we are to leverage what He's given us for the sake of His purposes. Gifts are intended to be *leveraged*. Your vocation is how you choose to leverage the gifts He's given you for the sake of the things He cares about.

In this section of the book, we're looking at identity. Your identity is partially made up of the gifts God has given you. These gifts may be spiritual gifts, supernatural abilities, or personality strengths. These come from God, and they're given freely to those who love Him. These gifts are blessings.

I've always been drawn to the parable of the talents, which talks about this. God gives each of us talents, which He intends for us to use. I have a friend who has an unbelievable talent. A serial entrepreneur, she can come up with crazy ideas, and every one of them succeeds. Her spiritual gift is the ability to start businesses and make money. She has a brilliant business mind—supernaturally so—but she recognizes God gave her the ability to do good in the world, not just reap the benefits of her talent. She now coaches entrepreneurs and gives away an exceptional amount of her resources because she knows gifts are intended to be leveraged for the good of the world.

Take an inventory of the abilities God has given you. What has God given you? The ability to encourage people? The ability to heal? Perhaps he's given you the ability to start businesses and make money. It sounds silly, but write the list down. Get a journal and make a bulleted list: What are all the abilities and spiritual gifts God has given you? Small, large, whether you think they're important and significant or not, add them to the list.

Perhaps this is one of the most important things we can do as we seek to find our stride, yet many of us get stuck here. We don't see our gifts as anything special. Maybe we want to remain humble. Maybe we've misunderstood humility. Here's a quick word to encourage you: Gifts matter. More specifically, your gifts matter. They've been given to you and are attached to your purpose. Whether you believe in Him or not, *Jesus believes in you,* and He's given you gifts for a reason.

When we take the time to list the gifts we've been given, we recognize the responsibility we have to *invest* them to serve the world. Bernie allowed us to serve others. We regularly carted our friends around and gave rides to those who needed them. What does it look like to invest your gifts for the sake of others? Once you've written a list of all the gifts He's given you, I encourage you to pray over each one and ask God, "Why?"

Chances are, His answer back to you will begin with two very specific words: "So that…"

… so that you can encourage others.
… so that you can empower others.
… so that you can serve others.
… so that you can equip others.

SELF-CONTROL

The challenge with gifts is that they can easily become idols. Have you ever seen your gifts, or the gifts of others, running over others and wreaking a path of destruction? What the Giver intended to bring life and hope can easily run entirely out of control and take advantage of others. Take finances, for example. Have you ever seen someone with resources facilitating corrupt systems and using wealth to lord it over others and take advantage of them? Sometimes, it's leadership skills that are intended to bless others but, instead, are used to facilitate one's own rise to the top on the backs of others. Gifts are intended to bring life, but without self-control and excellent steering, they have the potential to run over others.

Allow Bernie to illustrate. My sister and I thoroughly enjoyed the freedom that Bernie allowed. She was our prized possession because of the perks she allowed. We had friends who'd pile in regularly. We'd cruise to the grocery store for snacks any time we wanted. (We had a very innocent childhood. Yes, this was our definition of wild partying.) On our way to school one morning, we stopped at a local convenience store for the essentials—a donut and a Mountain Dew. In our haste, we quickly parked and ran inside because we only had a few minutes to get to school. After quickly checking out and heading back to the parking lot, we heard an old man scream, "It's headed for the furniture store!"

Blinded with our new-car joy and donut-based haste, we had neglected to engage the parking brake. The parking lot was on a giant hill, and to our horror, Bernie had transformed into an unguided missile. She was heading downhill through the very big and very steep parking lot and picking up steam. There was a busy road at the bottom of the shopping center and another shopping center on the other side. Bernie was on a suicide mission, and the likelihood of taking other lives with her was extremely high. We panicked (rightfully so!) and frantically called my dad. He answered, and before he could get a word out, we screamed, "Bernie's running away! She's out of control!"

"Slam on the brake!"

"We aren't in the car, Dad!"

Silence.

Our cherished gift was running away, carrying all our freedom, hopes, and dreams (and my completed homework). Bernie was a teacher, and I was the student. In my wild misfortune, I learned the importance of the e-brake.

The e-brake keeps you on the ground. The e-brake ensures your gift doesn't sail away with a mind of her own. In Luke 10:19–20, Jesus warns his disciples about this. They're so excited about the gifts and the newfound power they have. Jesus quickly corrects them: "The great triumph is not in your authority over evil but rather in God's authority over you and presence with you!" (The Message).

Our gifts and power can easily become a misguided missile, wreaking havoc and destruction everywhere they go. We've seen the same script act itself out over and over before us. It's almost predictable. When a person utilizes the gifts they've received, success comes, and their platform increases. Then, they idolize all the gifts God has given. Influence increases, and celebrity comes. Then, the destruction and the fallout come. So many leaders in the world have become wrecking machines of energy because they've forgotten to remain grounded.

As noted in this section's first chapter, we're grounded by our adoption. The e-brake of our lives is that we've taken His name and are no longer our own. The way to remain grounded when putting your gifts to use is to remember that you've been given a new name. As an adopted heir, the gifts you've received are tools to be utilized, not gods to be worshipped.

When we throw all our hopes and dreams on our gifts and forget to ground ourselves, our gifts become reckless. Yes, know your gifts, but don't set your hopes and dreams (or your homework) on them. And for God's sake, learn to embrace the e-brake. Gifts make a terrible god but a tremendous tool.

REFRAMING BLESSING

In Genesis 12, God spoke to Abraham and shared with him a vision for what his future would look like. He promised Abraham many descendants, a wild promise given that he didn't have a single child and was already old. God didn't just promise a child; He promised that Abraham's descendants would be as numerous as the stars in the sky and that the world would be *blessed* because of them.

I used to think that all gifts and blessings are the same thing, but they are not. However, all gifts can *become* blessings. A gift *becomes* a blessing when the benefactor is more than just the receiver.

This makes me think of a conversation I had with Jimi back on that trip. While on the multi-country trip, Jimi and I would debrief all we had seen and all that God appeared to be doing. Often, the discussions were heavy as we wrestled with the realities of refugees and vulnerable populations in this area of the world. On one particularly heavy day during the trip, Jimi told a story to provide a little levity and comedic relief. He shared about an activity he once did with his youth group back in the US.

He decided to do a pig chase with the kids. Jimi bought a pig, set up a circular fenced-in area, and instructed the kids to get ready. When the kids got in the ring, the pig looked confused. In fairness, he probably should have been. Jimi had handed the kids a tub of grease and told them to grease themselves up instead of the pig! It's the stuff of an HR director's nightmares. I can't imagine the number of letters the church must have received from parents, but as I reflected on it, maybe Jimi was on to something profound.

What if God doesn't give blessings to be chased, competed for, or captured? What if His blessings are more like a tub of grease to be spread? One by one, the kids dutifully obeyed the instruction, put some on their hands and arms, and then passed it along to the next person in the circle. It never ran out. In fact, like the loaves and fish, it seemed to multiply as it spread.

In God's economy, blessings have sacred importance. The spiritual adoption Doug received was a blessing when he used it as the basis for adopting others into the family. The disposition Mo had *became* a blessing when it was poured out for others. The gift of Bernie *became* a blessing when we used her to benefit others. Thanks to Jimi, I know that blessings are always intended to be spread.

As you take an inventory of all you've received—your unique identity, your name, your disposition, and your gifts—I want you to recognize that they are tools to be used for the benefit of others. They are not gods to be worshipped. Walk with confidence in your identity as a royal heir as you throw down all you've been given to build others up, and always remember to use the e-brake.

SECTION 5

DIRECTION

11

CURIOSITY OVER CLARITY

I used to think I needed all the details laid out in front of me. Now, I know that all I need is relentless curiosity.

Years ago, I took a group of people (particularly senior citizens) to a remote part of a Southeast Asian country that's not particularly friendly to Westerners. We had come to visit and encourage some friends who lived there and were planting a church. It's a very dangerous thing for them and could certainly lead to being dismissed from the country at best or imprisoned at worst.

I arrived separately from the rest of the team, and when I landed in the little country airport, no one was there to pick me up. No big deal. I've done a lot of international travel, so I didn't think twice about it. I began shuffling my papers to find a contact number while scanning the airport for a pay phone. (This was during the days when I didn't have a phone with international calling capacity yet.) With no payphones to be found, I tried to find an ATM to get some cash to pay a taxi driver but couldn't find one of those either. I decided to go back outside to scan the crowd again, as I was out of all other options. As I did, I was immediately surrounded by taxi drivers, all of whom were grabbing at my bags as I was swatting them away and immediately regretting my decision to go back outside.

Eventually, one of them handed me a flip phone—an open flip phone. I thanked him and began digging for the right contact info in my bag.

He interrupted me, put the phone up to my ear, and motioned for me to talk.

"Uh, hello?"

"Hey, JJ! We're so glad we got a hold of you," said the voice on the other end of the phone. He continued, "We have a little situation here; the man who was scheduled to pick you up was actually on his way there when he was arrested and taken in by the local authorities. So, we aren't showing our faces in public right now to ensure we aren't compromised in any way. Go with the guy who gave you this phone. He doesn't know a word of English, and he doesn't know what we're doing here, but we trust him. Go with him, and he'll bring you to us once it's safe."

Imagining my bride's face, if she only knew, I grabbed my bags and climbed into the back of his van, and we took off into the darkness of the jungle. It was nighttime. I had no way to communicate with the outside world, no cash, and no control over what was happening.

Eventually, we met up together, and after a night of sleep, we set out on the purpose of our trip: to explore how God is moving in remote islands where they're cut off from society, modern culture, and most world religions. We climbed into a roach-filled ferry, delirious from the mix of the jetlag, the sound of the engine, and the smell of the dirty exhaust smoke filling our lungs. The temperature was just under one million degrees Fahrenheit, and we had to stay on the ferry for at least three hours.

Just as I was truly going stir-crazy, the ferry stopped about two hundred yards from the shore and waited. We didn't know what to do, as the team was made up of mostly elderly individuals, and we all had our bags, overnight bags, and cameras. We just waited because we couldn't get out of the boat and swim to shore.

After a while, we saw a group of villagers on the shore who grabbed a handmade bamboo raft and paddled out to us. We all dutifully climbed out of the ferry onto the raft, cameras, bags, canes, and artificial hips in tow. Wobbly and worried, we waved goodbye to the ferry chugging on the distant horizon; we knew we were now alone. My friend (the one planting the church) knew the language and could communicate, but he had never visited this island before. We were in uncharted territory with no plan, strategy, accommodations, cell service, and now, no way to escape.

We spent several days on this island, building bridges of peace, connection, and service. We wanted to understand the lives of the people who lived here on this island, and they wanted to show us. We were overwhelmed by their tremendous hospitality, as we were invited to spend the evening in the home of the local village religious leader. We sat on his floor and ate fish and rice for dinner before setting up camp and sleeping on the concrete floor of his family room. He insisted we stay with him.

The next day, they wanted to take us on a "quick" three-mile hike inland to a waterfall that was apparently very beautiful. Six-and-a-half hours and many miles later, we finally made it. They had given us machetes to hack our way through the bush and to ward off any snakes. The trip included (literally) fire ants getting into my pants, many sleepless nights, raucous laughter, and redemption. We made new friends who (like us) were sojourners toward truth and spiritual understanding.

The whole trip, I struggled with feeling like we weren't doing *anything productive*. We weren't constructing a building, facilitating a medical clinic, teaching English lessons, or training pastors. We didn't plant crops or build clean water wells. We didn't have any formal plan; we just went with open hearts and curiosity. We asked questions and practiced the art of gratitude as they practiced hospitality. Somehow, I think we all learned more together about the Gospel of Jesus than we ever would have with a plan and strategy.

This brings us to the next section of our book: direction. As a coach, I have journeyed with hundreds of individuals who have felt like the clarity of their next season wasn't there. They felt stuck because they'd heard about the good works God had prepared in advance for them to do, but because they didn't know what those good works were yet, they concluded the best decision was to wait until there was clarity. Unfortunately, waiting almost always brings frustration.

It's helpful to think through the difference between a destination and a direction to move forward in the face of uncertainty. Allow me to unpack.

DESTINATION VS. DIRECTION

A destination is all about arrival. Many of us have built our faith on the idea of arrival: Where's our destination—Heaven or Hell? While this question is important, we've inadvertently allowed destination thinking to leak into other aspects of our journeys. We've allowed ourselves to only take steps if we know with clarity what the destination looks like. We only get on the ferry if we know where the nighttime accommodations are, what the planned activities are, and how we're getting back. This is because we've built our definition of success upon arrival at a destination.

Maybe we're exploring a new career, a new church, or a move to a new location. We want to know all the details and have a clear picture of what life will look like in the new reality before we step forward. When we go and look at a new house, we tour the house and *envision* family meals in the dining room, cooking in the kitchen, and playing with the kids in the yard. If we don't have a clear picture of what life will look like at the destination, we don't take steps forward in the process. Destination thinking is everywhere in our lives.

In contrast to destination thinking, consider direction. Direction is about moving along *the Way*. It's about the path. A direction focuses far more on the steps of obedience rather than arrival at any particular destination. The invitation of Jesus is to trust as we take steps forward on a path. Consider the calling of the disciples, which is recounted in Matthew 4:

> As Jesus was walking beside the Sea of Galilee, he saw two brothers, Simon called Peter and his brother Andrew. They were casting a net into the lake, for they were fishermen. "Come, follow me," Jesus said, "and I will send you out to fish for people." At once, they left their nets and followed him.
>
> Going on from there, he saw two other brothers, James, son of Zebedee, and his brother John. They were in a boat with their father Zebedee, preparing their nets. Jesus called them, and immediately, they left the boat and their father and followed him.

Notice the absence of details. The disciples weren't privy to the details. They didn't know what they'd do, where they'd go, how they'd provide, how much it would cost, or how long they'd be gone. The disciples were faced with a tremendous lack of clarity—and it was in that lack of clarity that they took action. They took steps when the future wasn't clear.

Most of us think of God's leading like a floodlight to our path. All the details will be illuminated if we're really called in a specific direction. We treat God like a glory-filled mapmaker who prides Himself on providing clear directions, illuminating all the steps and route in its entirety. With a great map, we can plod our way forward according to a perfect plan and avoid any missteps.

However, what if God doesn't lead that way? What if a better description of the light He provides is a lantern, illuminating just the next step or two and requiring our trust for what comes further down the line? Wouldn't He bring more glory to Himself through our obedience, then? Obedience requires trust in the face of the unknown. That's what we're invited to.

Finding a sacred direction does not have to be "knowing the plan and walking in it." It can be far more opportunistic than that. Sometimes, a sacred direction is as simple as, "Here's an opportunity, let's try it out. If this isn't the right path, God, please shut the door." You have the freedom to show initiative in discerning directions for your steps. *Try something.*

While there are times that God leads us by laying out all the steps in advance (Jonah, for example), I'm convinced that, more often, the path Jesus leads us toward is a little bit foggy. We struggle with this because clarity often carries the allure of safety. We treat clarity like a tool we need to move forward, but it's actually become an idol we're addicted to. In the mighty words of Mother Theresa, what if "clarity is the last thing we're holding on to"?

The most impactful individuals I've ever met always have something in common: They're relentlessly curious. Curiosity gets a bad rap in most Christian circles. It's almost as though, without clarity, our steps are somehow immature. "If this was really a mature thing to do, you'd have clarity." Or maybe it's a frugality mindset that scrutinizes everything and only wants to take a risk on a sure bet. In contrast, I think Jesus invites us to let curiosity and wonder lead the way as we take our next steps. What if you navigated future directions with curiosity and wonder instead of a master plan? What would look different?

The disciples may have had no idea where they were going, what they were doing, how long they'd be gone, or what it would cost, but they did know one thing: *They wanted to join Jesus in the direction He was headed.* So, they followed him. It reveals a truth that we'll unpack further in the next chapter: Direction is more about communion than it is about the arrival at a specific destination.

12

THE SUPPORTING CAST

I used to live like I was the main character. I found freedom when I realized I was not.

My beautiful bride, Shaina, has always loved Good Friday services. When we were engaged, we went to one that continues in our memories to this day. We made a last-minute decision to attend a service at a large mega-church in our town that was having a full theatrical performance for the evening. Thousands of audience members lined the interior of the giant auditorium. On the mammoth stage, there were dozens of actors, animals, and pyrotechnics, and the highest caliber musical numbers rose up from the orchestra pit below. It was really something. She and I were seated in the bleachers in the very back because we arrived a few minutes late. As a pastor's kid, I cherish sitting in the back any time I can, so the timing of our arrival was definitely intentional on my part.

We soaked up the entirety of the performance in all its somber glory. We saw the Last Supper play out in front of us. We felt anger against Judas as he betrayed Jesus with a kiss.

Our hearts broke with the injustice of the crown of thorns and the flogging of our Lord and Savior. We wept as He cried out, "It is finished!" then hung his lifeless head. The auditorium descended into dark, somber silence as the pastor got up and preached a quick message about the importance of living in our version of "Spiritual Saturday." All this happened before the glory picked up again as the music built toward the beautiful resurrection. We celebrated and cheered with the rest of the audience as everyone took a collective sigh of triumph.

I hate plays. I always have always will. However, there's something undeniably magical about watching a play about the passion week. When you take the perspective of an audience member watching a story unfold in front of you, you get to see a lot more of what's going on. You see Peter's inner turmoil when he's denied Christ three times and the rooster crows, but you also see the gentle kindness on the face of Jesus when he looks at Him in that moment.

It hit me as I was watching the story that instead of seeing things from a first-person perspective only, there's so much strength to pulling back and watching the story happening in front of us like we're in the audience, watching the characters move and interact before us. What if we could see the story of redemption being written in the lives of all those around us today? Maybe the best way to find our stride is to figure out what's going on in the lives of those around us and see where we can interject hope. The story is so much bigger than any of the disciples knew. The same is true today. If we want our lives to have the greatest impact, we have to try to align with the redemptive story God is writing.

MAIN CHARACTER PROBLEMS

While we intellectually know that it's not true, most of us act as though we're the main character in the story being written. As a result, we're riddled with anxiety, panic, worry, and concern over our future. We're paranoid about making a misstep because the world and our destiny seem to rest on our shoulders. What would look different about your life if you lived with a conscious awareness that the story is far bigger than you?

The best advice I can give anyone embarking on their next season is to quit living like you're the main character. You're not. When we understand that God is writing a redemptive story in the world, we can be more opportunistic in how we engage with it.

You're not the main character, but you're also not just an audience member. We have the option to jump in and play a role. You can be a supporting cast member. When we know that God is working, we have the option to join him in His work as characters within the story He's writing. Think of it less like a play and more like improv with a plot. We become influential characters in the story when we understand that we aren't the main character (He is!) and when we understand the Author's intent (what He's doing!). You and I have the option to jump in at any moment, utilizing all the skills, gifts, experiences, and capacities we have to help when we understand the direction the story is moving. We can be creative about how we put our skills to use for His purposes. You are free to put those skills to use wherever they'll have the greatest impact.

Think about the man who was casting out demons in Jesus's name. The disciples find this guy and tell him to stop. They go and report him to Jesus. What's Jesus's response? "Don't stop him! Whoever is not against us is with us!" This means that if you're aligned with what God is doing and working to bring glory to His name, you have the freedom and blessing to be creative with your actions. Finding the direction in our stride is simply laying our skill sets on the table wherever they may have the greatest impact. *Try stuff.*

THE IMPORTANCE OF COMMUNION

As we talked about in the last chapter, the disciples felt the courage to move forward without clarity *because they were with God.* The primary factor in discerning direction is communion with God. We need to ask the question, "Where's God?" Yes, he's everywhere, but if there's any trend we see in the Bible, it's that Jesus spent most of His time with the broken, the needy, and the lost. There's a clue there about what our direction should be. Discerning our direction should look a lot like communing with God where He's *already at work.*

In the story of the Passion Week, we see that Jesus was constantly on the move. Those in the story always had an option: join with him or do their own thing outside of Him. We have the same choice. While well-intentioned, many of us are self-focused and asking the wrong questions. We're asking God about His will for our lives. There's a better question to ask: *What's God's will in the world?* If we start by answering that, we can ask the second question: *How can I alter my life to fit into it?*

OBLIVIOUS TO THE PLOT

Back to the Good Friday performance. The play was beautiful, and before the cheering for the resurrection stopped, I nudged my (then) fiancé and suggested we beat the traffic and get to our car first. I may hate plays, but I'd been to a few. I know that what happens last is that the actors all line up while the audience does a standing ovation for about twenty minutes, and they'll bow over and over and over. I simply didn't have time for that.

We got to the back center door of the auditorium, and I put my hand on the handle to open it. Just then, three spotlights landed directly on me. Apparently, the music had been building to a crescendo, and I hadn't been paying attention. My plans were the priority. Now, unfortunately, I was the crescendo (not exactly visitor friendly!).

All eyes were on me in the huge auditorium of three thousand people. I just stood there paralyzed with my hand on the door handle. I didn't move. I couldn't move. I didn't know what in the world I had done to deserve this treatment. Shaina quickly disappeared back into the darkness.

Then, it happened. The doors flew open, and there in front of me was Jesus. In His full second-coming white-robed regalia, sitting triumphant with a sword atop an eight-foot-tall white horse, about to trample me down.

My plans and strategies were in direct opposition to where Jesus was moving. I wasn't wrong; I wasn't being sinful, destructive, or toxic. I just hadn't considered what He was doing. Most of us live our lives the same way. We make our decisions about direction based on tangible evidence and on our opinions and preferences, and we rarely consider what Jesus is up to. I had made an idol of clarity. I knew precisely where my car was and how long it'd take me to get there. I forgot about curiosity and was oblivious to what Jesus might have been up to. I was focused on my destination, getting home and getting to bed. I wasn't even considering joining Jesus in the direction He was moving.

From behind Jesus, an usher screamed, "Get out of the way! Get out of the way! You're ruining the second coming of Christ!" A lot of people have been accused of crazy stuff in the church, and rightfully so. However, I'm betting that I'm the first to be accused of this. I quickly dodged Jesus, ran through the lobby, and out to our car to drive home, totally humiliated. Amazingly, the girl still married me three months later. I think it was pity.

SECTION 6

ENDURANCE

13

MARATHON TRAINING

I used to want to rush the process. Now, I know that time is the secret ingredient to influence.

My original plan was to finish this book by running a marathon and writing about it. Wouldn't that have been an incredible ending? My inspiration lasted all of five days. During those five days, I went to Arizona and met with a friend there who is an ultra-marathoner. In fact, he *became* an ultra-marathoner in his seventies. He's incredible. I wanted some advice to determine if I have what it takes.

As a lifelong athlete with a passion for accomplishment and challenge, he decided he wanted a hobby. Someone told him if he could run two miles at an eight-minute pace, he could then just start adding miles at that pace. That's what he did. He began with running two miles, then three, and so on, always at the same pace. By the time I came into his life, the last race he had completed was a fifty miler, which began in the evening and lasted until the following afternoon. I asked about the path on these races, and he said it was a loop in a parking lot—a one-mile loop that he ran fifty times. My mind was blown. How on earth could anyone do this without going utterly insane?

I begged him to tell me his secret. What does he do to pass the time? What does he listen to, or what does he reflect on as he competes? His answer shocked me. He said, "Oh, no! I couldn't distract myself. I need to focus!" No music, no podcasts, no distraction from the pain. Instead, he leans in with focus. He wants to be present in his circumstances and power his way through the pain.

Admittedly, I didn't hear whatever it was he said next. I was too busy trying to determine whether he was man or machine. To be honest, I'm still not sure. But either way, he gave me a lot to think about. I drove away from our breakfast, realizing that marathon running would never be a part of my life, but maybe this kind of intentionality could be. I may not be tackling any ultramarathons (or marathons—or fun runs, for that matter), but I am tackling a vision for my future. I am working to find my stride and to utilize all that's been given to me to influence the world. His words were relevant to me, and I imagine they might also be to you.

At this point in the book, we've learned to unlock our unique story; we've identified our triggers, released the things we've been carrying, solidified our identity, and wrestled with our sense of direction. However, for many of us, there's still something missing. Many of us stop far earlier than we should, and it's a tragedy.

The sixth and final section of our stride is endurance. This is the missing component for us. Endurance is a long, drawn-out intentionality and focus—a steady commitment to forward progress over time.

For most of my life, my heroes have been those who've experienced a meteoric rise to success. I've idolized those at the top of their game and those who arrived there rapidly. Maybe you can relate. Our culture worships a meteoric rise.

What's interesting is that Jesus never really seemed to be drawn to a meteoric rise. In fact, maybe you recall the story of the rich young ruler recorded in the Gospels. Jesus meets the wunderkind and essentially tells him, "Hey, it's cool you want to follow me, but first go sell everything you've got. The accolades, trophies, and riches you've acquired are holding you back." (I'm paraphrasing—obviously.) He never fell into the admiration of the meteoric rise in others. Similarly, He never fell into its trap personally, either.

We live in an immediate society where everything is immediately available at the end of our fingertips, yet Jesus seemed to model something different: *patience*. It took about thirty years for Him to engage in any ministry work publicly. I've often wondered what this must have felt like for Mary, who knew the promises she had received about him before His birth but then waited day by day, nonstop, for thirty years, wondering if the time would ever come.

We need to find our stride by studying how Jesus found His, and one thing is completely clear: He wasn't in a rush. Jesus embodied patient endurance in His journey, and it's something we desperately need to imitate. Let's go deeper into what endurance looks like in our lives.

Endurance has three core components: sustained bite-sized movement, sustained narrow focus, and sustained audacious hope. Without any of these three components, our attempts at endurance are destined for failure. Let's unpack each at a deeper level.

SUSTAINED MOVEMENT

First, we need to look at the commitment to sustained bite-sized movement. This is the foundation of endurance. In Joshua 6, the Israelites were trying to determine their next steps while at the edge of Jericho. As articulated in the second verse, the

Lord began to speak to them: "Then, the Lord said to Joshua, 'See, I have delivered Jericho into your hands, along with its king and its fighting men.'"

While this was welcome news, the strategy that followed was perhaps a touch unconventional. God instructed them to march around the city once a day for six days, then on the seventh day, to do it seven times. Upon the completion of the march and a blowing of their trumpets, the city walls would fall. I've often wondered how Joshua felt hearing the strategy. Moreover, I wonder how his followers felt when he shared the plan with them! The brass section of the marching band probably saw it as their time to shine, but the warriors might have had some questions—not to mention the tiredness that would inevitably set in for everyone. They weren't even fighting yet, and already, this plan was exhausting.

"Joshua, if we keep marching like this, we're going to tire ourselves out!"

"Wouldn't we be far faster and more efficient if we dropped all this armor?"

When faced with a challenge of endurance, we're tempted by two options. We want to stop, or we want to sprint. God doesn't want us to do either. Instead, He invites us to commit to sustained bite-sized movement—foot in front of foot, a step at a time. God uses the monotony of movement to build our resilience, persistence, dependence, and more. When you find yourself doing repetitive things as you find your stride, you're in good company. God uses this repetition to build our resilience, strength, dependence on Him, and even our worship.

When my friend told me about the ultra-marathon races he did, the thing that blew me away was the one-mile loop—in a parking lot. There was no change of scenery and no trail. It sounds torturous. Maybe you're like me, and you thrive off change, and the idea of the same monotonous thing for miles strikes you as cruel and unusual punishment. One of the things we learn in the march of the Israelites is that they overthrew Jericho led by worshippers, not by warriors. God is up to something in the monotony of repetition. Don't stop or sprint through it; worship your way through the monotony.

SUSTAINED FOCUS

Next, we need to look at sustained, narrow focus. The thing that made me conclude my friend was more machine than man was that he said he could afford no distractions. I'd give anything for a distraction. Isn't that a survival technique in a race like that?

One of the biggest challenges of endurance is the monotonous nature of progress and our tendency toward distraction. I think again of the Israelites wandering through the desert, which was a mind-numbing task spread out over forty years. Have you ever noticed how often they were distracted and threw their allegiance to idols? Every time Moses went up on a mountain to meet with God, he came down to find the Israelites with a golden calf. I find myself in the journey of the Israelites, and maybe you do, too. Tired of the monotony, boredom leads to distraction, and distraction leads to the construction of idols—lesser gods we think we can control. It might not be a golden calf, but greater financial success, power, or image. When we're bored with faithfulness, we escape through distraction. We need a strategy to maintain long-term faithfulness and keep our focus on the horizon.

The other thing about distraction is that it far too easily becomes an escape. Distraction numbs the mind, and in doing so, it makes us less present. You're not fully present if your mind is somewhere else (somewhere ideally a bit less painful!). Maybe my friend had a point, despite how uncomfortable I was with it.

Sustained narrow focus is a choice, one we must commit to. It's hard, and I often catch my mind wandering. It's a helpful discipline to practice presence, even in trivial things. The task is to keep our minds present in the journey in front of us. Most of us multi-task everything—our parenting, relationships, even our vocation. By practicing single-tasking for shorter periods and taking intentional breaks to catch our breath, we can function with much higher focus and intentionality in our lives. This is where habits can be immensely helpful. If we build habits—daily rhythms to reground us in the importance of our calling and communion with Him—we will begin to see results and build our endurance simultaneously. Practicing presence is hard, but presence is the key to impact.

SUSTAINED HOPE

Last is sustained audacious hope. Looking to the good works God prepared in advance for us to do, we need to understand that hope is the fuel to bring those dreams to fruition. The great temptations we face when journeying toward our future are despair and cynicism. In Genesis 12, there's an incredible promise that God gave to Abraham (at the time, his name was Abram):

> The Lord had said to Abram, "Go from your country, your people, and your father's household to the land I will show you. I will make you into a great nation, and I will bless you; I will make your name great, and you will be a blessing. I will bless those who bless you, and whoever curses you I will curse, and all peoples on earth will be blessed through you."

God made this promise to Abram at a time when he had no kids. Both he and his wife were already well past child-bearing years, and God made this audacious promise for descendants that would make up a great nation. That's the thing about God-sized visions: They're always audacious. God has never presented a small vision or an otherwise achievable plan; He specializes in the impossible. This is important to understand because as you seek to discern the steps toward your future, you need to understand that if God's in it, it probably won't feel tame. It won't feel doable. It might feel impossible. Pay attention when it feels that way; it might just be His calling.

As God presented Abram with a seemingly impossible but delightful vision, Abram only saw the reasons it wouldn't work. He looked at the circumstances around him, and he chose cynicism. He said that it couldn't be done. Sustained audacious hope is only possible when we choose to trust even though our circumstances look bleak. Sadly, Abram took matters into his own hands, claiming the promise of God on his life but taking control of how it came about. He chose the path to descendants that was most logical: He slept with one of his servants. He wanted to claim the promise of blessing in his life, but he concluded God needed some help in bringing it to fruition. Abram made his choice based on impatience and doubt. I do the same thing constantly, and maybe you do, too. Where are you allowing cynicism, impatience, and doubt to shape your actions about the future?

The example of Abram shows us that it's not enough to claim the promise of God over our lives and then try to maneuver our way to His blessings on our terms. Instead, hope, trust, and faithfulness are choices we must make. As you look to find your stride and navigate your next steps—through your career, vocation, and relationships—how can you replace your cynicism, impatience, and doubt with faithfulness, trust, and audacious hope?

Scripture teaches us that hope is the key to endurance. Hope becomes the source of energy and sustained life force that moves us forward. Isaiah 40:31 says, "Those who hope in the Lord will renew their strength. They will soar on wings like eagles; they will run and not grow weary; they will walk and not be faint."

If we learn anything from him, we must understand that sustained audacious hope must be chosen. It doesn't happen naturally. Instead, it's a commitment we make, just like forward progress. Commit to choosing hope at all costs and avoiding despair.

THE IMPORTANCE OF TIME

Ask any chef what their secret ingredient is; they probably won't tell you. The good news for you is I'll tell you: It's *time*. Time is their magic ingredient. Have you ever tried to speed things up when you're cooking Thanksgiving dinner? You turn the temperature in the oven up to save a few minutes, and you burn the turkey on the outside and have a raw inside. We did that a few years ago, so I speak from experience. You try to speed up your influence in the world, and you end up burnt on the outside and ripped raw inside.

Time breaks down things that are tough and makes them tender and succulent. Time and pressure acting together break down the tough sinews of the heart and bring about something beautiful. It's amazing how cooking speaks to our spiritual health, as well. Time is the magic ingredient that transforms. Time is also the thing that makes others hungry. Want a fragrance to arise that makes those around you salivate for the hope you have? Model faithfulness and gentleness over *time*.

My friend Greg knows this well. I got to know Greg years ago down in Arizona. He has an interesting story. He was a successful banker for his entire career. In fact, he was in the C-suite of a global bank and was at the top of his game. The only problem was that he wasn't happy.

Greg had long had a passion for art. He was a hobby painter and had a natural affinity for it. He began to be drawn to the thought of painting as his career. He talked with his friends and colleagues and told them he was making a ten-year plan to exit the banking world and become a performance painter full-time. Ten years is far longer than most of us would be willing to invest in a new strategy or plan, but Greg has given me a new perspective on endurance. Ten years later, almost to the day, Greg walked out of his office and into his future.

As we look to find our stride and uncover the things God has prepared for us to do, we need to ask: *What am I willing to endure for?* Greg stayed in banking until he had a vision that he knew he was willing to sacrifice years of his life for. While ten years seems like a very long time to invest, we need to remember that Jesus took thirty before he did the good works God the Father had prepared for him to do. We need to look at all our time investments in light of eternity. Considering eternity, ten years doesn't seem so bad at all.

The challenging thing about time is that our minds play tricks on us. I have a confession: Remember, in the first chapter of this book, I talked about a run with Chris that was almost doubly as long as he originally mentioned? It was only an 8K. I had prepped for a 5K. It wasn't a marathon. It wasn't an Ironman. Yet, that's how it *felt to me.* Our emotions can play strong tricks on us. In the throes of battle, it can feel like we've been at war for years, even if it's just been a few minutes. As we take steps toward the future we desire, it can feel like a marathon, but in the grand reality of eternity, it's but a moment in time.

When God Slows Us Down

As I write this morning, it's December 9, and I'm sitting in a leather chair looking out my window at the snow-covered beauty of God's creation. It keeps my attention for about ten seconds before I'm distracted by the draw of the phone in my pocket and the sound of little feet bounding down the stairs.

Also, as I write this morning, my foot is elevated with ice. I broke it. I'm unable to put weight on it for weeks. Every person who sees me hobbling around on crutches or rolling around on my scooter asks the same question: "How'd you do it?"

Sadly, I must admit the details. I was trying to impress my beautiful bride and our two boys. I told her, "Hey babe, watch this…" (which apparently is the precursor for injuries at age forty). We were playing soccer together, and I attempted to kick the ball out of the air and impress the masses around me. Instead, I missed the ball with all the grace of a car crash, landed on my foot the wrong way, and collapsed into a painful pile of forty-year-old mush.

It's impossible to move fast on crutches. You can go slightly faster on a scooter, but not much (though it hasn't stopped me from attempting to make skid marks from tight turns on the kitchen floor). You can't do anything fast on these things; everything is slow and calculated. In fact, I think I did a seventeen-point turn on the scooter yesterday—*sustained bite-sized movement.*

You also can't multi-task. Each movement has a purpose. It takes my full attention to get a snack from the kitchen and bring it to the family room. Don't even get me started on the level of planning and coordination required to take a shower. Suddenly, the things I could multi-task through have become things I need to single-task on—*sustained narrow focus.*

When the doctor told me I'd have to have a boot on for weeks and that if I was faithful to his plan, there was a chance I might not need surgery, it was music to my ears. Surgery makes me anxious. I'm not normally one for following the rules, but when he laid them out, I hung onto every word. "If it means no surgery, I'll do it!" The possibility of a surgery-free recovery was just the vision I needed to be faithful with this non-weight-bearing purgatory and to tolerate the stupid boot and nighttime splint daily for weeks—*sustained audacious hope.*

It's almost as if God knows that I might think I can sprint my way through His Advent but that there's much more in store for me if I don't. Instead, I must choose Him or something else. I might think that the feeling of productivity is more important than my presence, but it's not.

Our calling cannot be rushed or multi-tasked through despite our best intentions. We're often so eager to get to the sweet spot. We're so eager to find our "made for this moment" that we rush through the process. Yet, God's invitation is patience and endurance—specifically because patience leads to progress when done with faithfulness. Where are you rushing the process? What does it look like for you to commit to sustained bite-sized movement, sustained narrow focus, and sustained audacious hope? Endurance is the key to getting where God has designed you to be.

14

SANDCASTLES AND TIDAL WAVES

—◇—

I used to see God's footprints in the sand. Now, I see them in the whitewater.

Remember that poem about the footprints in the sand? Surely, you've seen it in a greeting card store or a Christian bookstore. "There were two sets of footprints in the sand," the author says when comparing his walk with the Lord to a walk on the beach. The poem goes on to describe how the two sets drop down to one, and the idea represents the times in our lives when God carries us. It's a beautiful sentiment that's hanging on family room walls or in framed pictures in bathrooms all throughout the world. The image is always the same: a peaceful beach with a sunset over the gently lapping, calm waters. I used to think that'd be the description of my journey—a walk on the beach. I learned early that wasn't the case.

My dad has always been passionate about adventure and "bending" (ignoring) the rules. Anytime there was a sign warning of danger, he viewed it as a personal invitation. I love him for that, though it's always terrified me at the moment.

I remember a vacation on a beachside campground in California as a kid. It was an amazing vacation at a campsite right on the cliffs overlooking the water. I'm sure it's since gone, replaced with multi-million-dollar mansions, but at the time, it was a little boy's dream—a sandy, dirty, smoky paradise. We spent all day hanging out, and then the evenings were spent grilling hotdogs, making smores, playing games, and telling wacky stories. I don't think I showered, period. Dirty, smelly, little boy bliss. It was perfect.

The main beach we'd hang at had a cliff next to it that jutted out far into the water with a big no-trespassing sign. Then, there was supposedly another beach on the other side of the cliff. My older sister and I were perfectly content playing in the sand and building our castles. Dad, however, was not. Outside of my mother's earshot, he invited us on an adventure to journey through the water on the front face of the cliff and make our way over to the beach on the other side. My sister was tentatively open to the idea, but I didn't want to go. This beach was fine. It was *comfortable*. I could continue building my castles in the sands of contentment. Dad argued back that yes, this beach was comfortable, but that beach over *there* was *great*.

Sure, there may have been another path to get there, but it wasn't just about the arrival at the other beach. The invitation was to an adventure. Dad reminded me, "*Son, we are made for more! We are made to be adventurers!*" In that moment, Dad shaped a foundational truth to my faith journey, which applies to all of us: Jesus is never content to leave us where we are. It's a tragedy when we let the comfort and convenience of what *is* keep us from what He's leading us *toward*.

Comfort and convenience are the enemies of meaning. Breaking away from convenience is incredibly hard. We talked about it earlier, but the power of inertia is great. An object (or human) at rest will stay exactly where they are unless there's a catalyst. The greatest threat to the story that *could be* is the convenience of what *is*. I was more than content to keep building castles in the sand. Maybe that's you. Maybe you're content building your castles and building your kingdom with what you have, and God's inviting you to consider a greater adventure with Him. The journey to embracing a life of greater purpose always involves *a catalyst*.

Sometimes, the catalyst is obvious—a challenge from your dad, a job loss, a cancer diagnosis, the death of a loved one, a mysteriously burning bush, an invitation from a mysterious Rabbi walking along the beach, or some other powerful moment in our lives.

I talked to a woman last week who lost her son unexpectedly and tragically thirteen years ago. She said that right after it happened, she was paralyzed. Stuck. The world she had known and been comfortable in was suddenly flipped upside down, and there was no way of making sense of it. That's a trajectory-altering event. It became a catalyst in her life, and she realized that she could help change the lives of many other families by leaning into the loss she had experienced. She and her husband started a foundation to help others find hope and peace and to avoid similar tragedies. They've since helped thousands of families.

Sometimes, it's not a one-time event but far more subtle—a slow-growing discontent in your soul. I talked to a friend just yesterday who said that God's been building a discontent in him for the last two years that's all centered around one word: *comfort*. He said that God invited him to take an adventure, but God has clarified that comfort won't be part of the equation. If we want greater meaning in our lives, chances are God is calling us to get comfortable with being uncomfortable.

Back to the adventure at the beach. We set off on Dad's crazy journey, and my older sister went with us, too. We made our way along the edge of the base of the cliff to the point that was farthest out in the water. We walked along the side of the cliff until I couldn't touch the ground anymore; then, I began swimming as we approached the corner that would bring us along the rock face that was farthest out. Dad reassured me that I was a good swimmer, so there was nothing to worry about.

"Hey, Dad, should we let that wave pass us first before we go?"

"Nah, it's a long way off."

Spoiler alert: It wasn't. It was coming, and it was coming fast. A huge rogue wave was approaching with the force of a freight train, and it had no interest in stopping for us. At the last second, Dad grabbed our hands. The wave smashed over us and threw us against the rock. There was whitewater everywhere.

Have you ever noticed that stepping out with Jesus to a life of greater purpose and meaning is not easy? The journey of joining Jesus in a crazy adventure is rarely, if ever, easy. There are twists and turns. There's *whitewater*. Many of us think that the walk with Jesus toward a greater purpose will be #blessed. When we don't experience the blessing, we often wonder what we did to anger God. When we step out with God, we often imagine receiving his favor and kindness, so if/when we don't, we question. Perhaps we didn't hear Him, right? Perhaps this wasn't the plan? Perhaps He just doesn't like us? If we aren't blessed, what are we? Are we not in His will?

I'm reminded of Psalms 13:1–2, which says, "How long, oh, Lord? Will you forget me forever? How long will you hide your face from me? How long must I wrestle with my thoughts and day after day have sorrow in my heart? How long will my enemy triumph over me?"

Getting crushed by a wave is a horrible feeling. First, it's the terrifying sensation of attempting to find your footing while being lifted off your feet by the momentum. Then comes the crash. The breaker crashes upon you and folds your body up like a pretzel underwater, twisting and turning as the saltwater infiltrates your nostrils, stinging like a sinus infection. Eventually, the wave subsides, and while you're still trying to catch your breath and gain your bearings, you face the greatest danger—the prospect of being sucked out to sea.

The waves of life are sneaky, and there's a huge importance to this. The real danger exists in a way that many of us are clueless about. When the pain in our story comes—when the divorce comes, when the death of a loved one comes, when the cancer diagnosis comes, when disappointment or hurt feelings happen—it's not just the pain itself that's the problem. Yes, it hurts, but the true and greatest danger is that it can drag us permanently off course. I've seen this pattern in my life and observed it in the lives of many others. When pain comes, it's easy to feel bewildered, broken, and even bitter. Our pain can become the defining story of our lives and permanently throw us off the journey Jesus wants to lead us through.

Where's the whitewater in your life? Do you resonate with this? Have the circumstances thrown you in your life?

In recent years, I've found myself reflecting on Psalm 42. It's a curious passage, as verse 7 says, "Deep calls to deep, in the roar of your waterfalls; all your waves and breakers have swept over me."

It sounds a bit like drowning, doesn't it? Why would the psalmist describe God's relationship with him as waves and breakers crashing over him? Maybe you're in the whitewater of life at this moment, working to find your stride and taking steps of obedience. Yet, the chaos of life has hit you like a rogue wave. As you're tossed and turned and violently thrown,

I want you to remember the words of Psalm 42, particularly the first five words: *"As deep calls to deep."*

What if the whitewater is an invitation to fellowship? Jesus knows what it is like to be in the chaos and whitewater of life. Is there any pain that we can be brought into that He has not endured? No. Suffering is our invitation for fellowship with Him. His presence meets us there. The invitation of Jesus to a life of greater purpose is an invitation to greater *communion* with Him as we navigate the waves and whitewater of life.

One of my all-time favorite passages is Matthew 14: 22–33. It's the story of Jesus and Peter walking on water, and it carries profound insights for us.

> Immediately, Jesus made the disciples get into the boat and go on ahead of him to the other side while he dismissed the crowd. After he had dismissed them, he went up on a mountainside by himself to pray. Later that night, he was there alone, and the boat was already a considerable distance from land, buffeted by the waves because the wind was against it.

> Shortly before dawn, Jesus went out to them, walking on the lake. When the disciples saw him walking on the lake, they were terrified. "It's a ghost," they said and cried out in fear.

> But Jesus immediately said to them: "Take courage! It is I. Don't be afraid."

> "Lord, if it's you," Peter replied, "tell me to come to you on the water."

> "Come," he said.

Then Peter got down out of the boat, walked on the water, and came toward Jesus. But when he saw the wind, he was afraid and, beginning to sink, cried out, "Lord, save me!"

Immediately, Jesus reached out his hand and caught him. "You of little faith," he said, "why did you doubt?"

And when they climbed into the boat, the wind died down. Then, those who were in the boat worshiped him, saying, "Truly you are the Son of God."

This story offers many insights for us. The story begins with Jesus sending the disciples out in a boat into the darkness, seemingly without him. Interestingly, the story happens just after the miraculous feeding of the five thousand. The disciples have just been a part of one of the greatest miracles of all time: They've split a few fish to feed thousands. Then, they're sent off to the great unknown.

"This all smells a bit fishy to me," says Peter. "Nah, it's just the fish guts," murmur the others under their breath.

Most of us think about the calling of God this way. We envision being sent off into the great unknown, that it all hinges on us, and that we're alone, operating as sent-but-sent-alone ones. Maybe this is you. Maybe you feel He's launching you off to the great unknown. The hope we find in the story is that Jesus shows up even when we think He's not there. There's nowhere you can go that's outside of His reach and presence. Go with courage that He is there.

This brings us to the second insight from the story—Jesus's location. We need to recognize Jesus's location in the story. *He's not in the boat.* It's a basic observation, but it's an important consideration. Jesus is out in the darkness, the whitewater, the wind, and the waves. From there, He instructs Peter to join

Him, which leads us to our next insight: The call to step out is a call to communion. Don't make the mistake of thinking you're stepping into a new adventure alone. You're not. God is already there, and He's inviting you to join him.

Next, the call to step out is a call to risk. When we're considering taking a step forward toward greater meaning, impact, and influence in the world, it often looks like embracing greater risk.

Finally, the call to step out is a call to greater dependence. If you wonder what your future steps should look like, consider where will put you in a position of greater dependence on Him. It was windy, dark, and stormy. Opportunities to risk rarely come when it's calm; they usually come when there's chaos.

BACK TO THE SEA

As the giant wave smashed off the rock and began to recede out to sea, we clung to the rock with everything we had. Technically, Dad clung to the rock, and he also clung to us. What a visual. Yes, he was the one who created this whole situation in the first place, but man, Dad was giving us some powerful sermon illustrations. It's almost like this was all part of his master plan.

A quote often attributed to Charles Spurgeon reads "I have learned to kiss the wave that throws me against the Rock of Ages." The trials of life, our pain, and our suffering are all catalysts for greater intimacy with God, but the temptation is to view waves as the enemy. Most of us don't go out searching for whitewater. We don't seek challenges in life. However, if we never risk, we'll never experience intimacy with Him, and we will never be put in a situation where we must cling to the Rock. We must develop a theology of risk, a spiritual framework by which we view risk as something of value. We have to recognize that a life with Jesus is not a life of comfort and ease; it's a life of adventure, which means the hits will come.

Jesus intentionally invites us to unsafe situations because it brings us into fellowship with Him. Listen for His voice if you've allowed your spiritual walk to get comfortable, convenient, and safe. It probably sounds a bit like my dad's: "*Son, we are made for more. We are made to be adventurers!*"

Our stride is found at the intersection of our story, our triggers, the things we must release, our identity, our direction, and our endurance. I pray that you step mightily toward all the good works God has prepared in advance for your future. However, please know this: The journey probably won't look like a walk on the beach; chances are it looks like joining Him in the whitewater.

As soon as the wave receded, Dad was embarrassed, and the very first words out of his mouth were the three words every child knows so well—not "I love you" but "Don't tell Mom." The first thing we did was cry and go tell Mom.

WALKING NOT RUNNING

Now that we've worked through all the components of finding our stride, it's off to the races, right? I've been mulling this over as I've prepared to write the end of this book. We have unlocked our stories, identified our triggers, released the things we've been carrying, defined our identities, oriented around a direction, and committed to endurance. However, maybe something still feels like it's missing. It did for me. So, I went for a walk to pray it over.

Here's what struck me: Walking also has a stride.

We often build up narratives in our heads about those who have found their strides. We conclude that they're running ahead, unhindered, racing forward in world impact. I had mistakenly formed an idea that I'd be running to win once I found my stride. However, maybe my stride will look like walking, not running, step by step into my future.

My thoughts turned to the story of Jesus and the paralytic in Mark 2. Maybe you remember the story. Jesus is preaching in a home, and it's running late. It's jam-packed, and everyone is hanging onto his every word. Then, there's a noise coming from the ceiling. A paralytic and some of his friends have come up with a crazy plan to get to Jesus. They're digging through the ceiling; drywall and dust descend on the head of the Almighty. Unphased, Jesus doesn't seem to care. Perhaps the hammering and sawing may have distracted the crowd, but He is still preaching strong. Then, the crowd notices a man on his mat being lowered from the ceiling. It's probably hard to preach through that. Eventually, the noises subside, and it's quiet and still as the eyes of the masses are on Jesus and the paralytic hanging on a mat in front of him.

I've often wondered about the paralytic. It takes an awful lot to dream that Jesus may just be the key that can bring healing, hope, and dry bones to life. Maybe he's tried all other options, and everything has left him dissatisfied. He's seen everyone else around him walking and running for years, moving forward in their lives with joy, meaning, and purpose, yet he's felt stuck. Maybe you can relate. Maybe you've been looking at those around you, envious of the stride they appear to have found. You want a life of purpose and meaning and to embrace the good works God has designed you for, but you've felt stuck, trapped, and paralyzed.

Here's the thing: Jesus looks at the man and is *moved by his faith*.

It's not enough to unlock your story, identify your triggers, release the things you need to release, solidify your identity, discern your direction, and commit to endurance. There's one more step. You need to have faith that you can—with His help—live a different story.

Then, in verse 11, comes the magic invitation from the Savior, which carries the same weight for you and me today: "Take up your mat and *walk.*"

EPILOGUE

As I've already mentioned, Chris and I did that lakefront jog in Chicago. In it, I learned how to move easily and with the least friction. Chris is still a runner; I am still not, though I've learned the art of walking. I walk numerous miles daily, and it's become a source of peace. Can one have a walker's high? If so, I think I've got it.

Annabelle is thriving in her organization, and we've partnered on many different initiatives during the last two years. Most recently, we started a home for survivors of trafficking. It's called the Jewels of Honor shelter in Kampala, Uganda. Over thirty girls, ages eight to eighteen, have come through the home.

Sahar continues leading her medical clinic for refugees in Greece. The war in Ukraine has continued to open the floodgates of displaced people into Greece. We've worked together to develop an ESL initiative, a job training initiative, and an officially licensed Greek clinic caring for many refugees.

The Lesvos camp has folded. It burned down in a fire a couple of years ago. It's now been replaced by other camps scattered throughout Greece. We spent time connecting with refugees in the biblical city of Corinth, where there are two camps. Each one carries horrors and atrocities, but the hope of Jesus is spreading within them like wildfire.

To learn more about these incredible ministry initiatives, go to www.compelglobal.org/donate and scroll down the page. One hundred percent of financial investments given to these ministries go directly to the projects on the ground.

The school for children in Nazareth is still there, and even with the war, it's still thriving. Go to www.lovedoes.org to learn more.

All the stories in the book have additional details that haven't made it into the chapters, so I want to share some of them here.

We returned to the Candy Kitchen years later as a family. My sisters decided to play a trick on me, and they talked to the manager (without my knowledge) and told Him what had happened years earlier. Then, as I stood in the store perusing the options, the manager came up to me and immediately forced me out. Shocked that he'd know who I was, I begrudgingly obliged—and got the giggles again. Old habits die hard.

Remember how Greg shaped a ten-year plan to leave his career in banking? Ten years later, almost to the day, he walked out of his banking office with a box of his things, his nameplate, and a huge smile on his face. He walked straight into a new career as a full-time performance painter, performing portraits and other paintings done to music on stage. He's performed for the Olympic opening ceremonies, conferences done by Apple and Google, and more. Greg is a world-renowned painter who has raised over 1 million dollars for charity through his auctioned paintings. Endurance wins in the end!

One other story needs more explanation: Bernie's death mission. As I left it in the chapter, Bernie was careening out of control down the steeply sloped parking lot to a busy road and second parking lot with a store down below. As we stood helpless in the parking lot above, cars continued moving along, generally undisturbed, but aside from one small ding against another parked car, she made it through the top parking lot all right. Heading down toward the road, we frantically prayed, "Jesus, you've truly got to take the wheel!" She was going about forty miles per hour and easily could have killed someone. She crossed the road through several lanes of traffic without hitting a soul! She careened through the bottom parking lot toward a furniture store, made a slight turn, and came to a complete stop—in a parking spot, perfectly between two white lines with two cars in the spots next to her.

To this day, it's the best parking job I've ever done.

When it seems that all control is lost and like we're careening out of control, and there's no hope for our futures, sometimes, the best strategy we can have is prayer—and then we watch. We watch how God steers, moves, and morphs us to eventually fit into the exact right spot in the exact right place at the exact right time.

If cars could think, I bet Bernie was thinking, *Whoa! What a ride! I made it exactly where I'm supposed to be!* My friends, I hope your path looks quite different than Bernie's, but I pray you share the same conclusion at the end.

FIND YOUR STRIDE

workbook

JOSIAH HARLING

Ready to take things further?
Go to <u>findingyourstride.pro/workbook</u>
and get started on your future today!

ACKNOWLEDGEMENTS

So many voices have shaped the stories in this book, I'm almost hesitant to list anyone for fear of who I'll forget. To everyone who has influenced me (whether your names are mentioned in the pages or not), you've taught me more about the character and heart of God than I could ever describe.

Shaina, Joshua, and Theo – living out the journey of following Jesus together with you is the honor of a lifetime. I love the way you live your faith out loud – keep it up, the world is noticing. Thanks for your interest in what I've been writing, thanks for asking questions, and most of all thanks for loving me regardless of what I succeed in or fail in. The way you love me teaches me about Jesus.

Mom and Dad, you've taught me so much about chasing the heart of God and finding purpose in serving others. Thank you. Thanks for the constant willingness to review the pages I've written, then reread them as I move from draft to draft, all without losing an ounce of enthusiasm. That means so much to me!

To the rest of my family, friends, and coworkers – thank you.

Chris O'Byrne and the team at Jetlaunch Publishing, thanks for all of your help, it's an honor to partner together. Keri Spring, thanks for believing in the impact of this book. It's meant a ton.

THE FLOP
PODCAST

FAILURE IS THE BEST TEACHER.

LEARN FROM YOUR BIG FLOPS.

JETLAUNCH.LINK/THEFLOP

Printed in the USA
CPSIA information can be obtained
at www.ICGtesting.com
JSHW081926180924
69889JS00002B/62